Radio in My Soul

Radio in My Soul:
The Journey of James "Dr. Daddio" Walker

James Walker
with Misti Aas

DALAYO PUBLISHING

Radio in My Soul: The Journey of James "Dr. Daddio" Walker
Copyright © 2022 by James Walker with Misti Aas

Published by Dalayo Publishing

ISBN 979-8-9871792-2-2 (paperback)
ISBN 979-8-9871792-1-5 (ebook)

Cover & Interior design by Sara Schaller at Designs by Seraphim
Edited by Scott Reynolds

This book is dedicated in memory of the three amazing women who shaped my life: my mother, Mattie (Ludie) Frazier-Walker; my sister, Minnie Walker-Dawson; and my wife, Patsy Ruth Stroman-Walker.

Author Note

This book is a true story based on my best and honest recollections of the events of my life through my own frame of reference, with some added expansion and research from my co-author. We aimed for truth and accuracy; any discrepancies in facts or memories are accidental. This memoir is not intended to cover every aspect of the vast and varied experiences in my journey. Rather, it is a collection of a few of those key moments that have shaped who I am. There are many important people in both my past and present I did not have the opportunity to mention inside this text, and these vital individuals are no less important to where I am now. This unfolding of my narrative has meaning for me beyond measure.

Table of Contents

Foreword by brother jeff   i

1   Introduction   1

2   Arriving in Five Points   4

3   Early Radio: Path to Houston   7

4   Hamm's Brewing Company   11

5   Growing up in Gibsland   13

6   Patsy   19

7   Beginning in Denver and the KDKO Journey   23

8   Promoting   32

9   Tucson   49

10   KDKO Ownership   55

11   Daddio's Kitchen on Wheels   64

12   Sturgis   71

13   Ongoing RV Journey   74

14   Radio Post KDKO:
KUVO and AM 760 Progressive Talk Radio   80

15   Fair Share Jobs   85

16	Asphalt Sealant Business	93
17	Artesian Water Business	97
18	Youth Fishing Trips	102
	Pictures	106
19	Race and Discrimination	156
20	God's Role in My Life	171
21	Motivation	184
22	Capturing History and Stories	190
23	Notable Names	203
24	Five Points	227
	Afterword	242
	Words From My Children	245
	References	264
	Acknowledgments	269

Foreword by brother jeff

Two words define James "Dr. Daddio" Walker–legend and legacy. Few are living legends, and fewer create meaningful legacies. Dr. Daddio is both. This giant instilled in me the responsibility of giving people their flowers while they can smell them. These opening words are my bouquet to a man who has been a father, role model and mentor to me and countless others.

The Walker home was a place where I formed many of my fondest childhood memories. I grew up playing with the Walker siblings while listening to Dr. Daddio on KDKO Radio and becoming part of the family. I am very familiar with the stories told within this memoir. They hold a special place in my heart, and I am excited Dr. Daddio has shared them in book form.

Beyond the inspirational stories is Dr. Daddio's blueprint for success and an example of family values rooted in faith, education and directing one's own destiny. His blueprint has worked for me and guides my life and success. I remember Dr. Daddio coming home as a KDKO employee who purchased the station as a family business and employed the Black community. From a Denver, Colorado vantage point, Dr. Daddio is known for owning KDKO radio. However, looking from the other side of the Rocky Mountains, he is further noted as an Arizona radio station owner.

Radio station ownership is only a part of Dr. Daddio's business legacy. He also owned Dr. Daddio's Kitchen on Wheels, BBQ restaurants, water and asphalt businesses, and provided community service by creating Fair Share Jobs, an agency devoted to closing the Black employment gap.

As a young entrepreneur, working for Dr. Daddio at KDKO shaped my business acumen. He overcame systemic barriers to Black radio station ownership and never missed a payroll. I was an on-air personality, served in key roles within the management structure, and ran the KDKO internship program. Many of today's top radio talent got their start with Dr. Daddio.

I have had a front-row seat to Dr. Daddio's life. He has been a successful promoter with friends like James Brown, The Jackson Five, Gladys Knight, Bobby Blue Bland, and B.B. King, to name a few. With an incredible ear for musical talent, he played a key role in securing Denver natives as founding members of Earth Wind and Fire.

A man of faith, I witnessed his installation as a church deacon, was supportive when he buried his older sister, and was with Dr. Daddio and the Walker family during the passing and burial of his soulmate and wife, Patsy.

Much of what I do in business, community and in life is simply a reflection and tribute to Dr. Daddio, who taught me the value of hard work, never giving up on my dreams, and being bold while speaking truth to power. When you see me, you see him. I am honored and proud to be a part of Dr. Daddio's legacy. He has had a profound impact on my life, and I am sure there are many ways in which Dr. Daddio has also shaped your life.

Dr. Daddio's life is one of love whose message we can sum up in his mantra, Unity in the Community.

1 | Introduction

ıı||ıı||ıı||ı 🎙 ıı||ıı||ıı||ı

"The ultimate measure of a man is not where he stands in moments of comfort and convenience, but where he stands at times of challenge and controversy."

- Dr. Martin Luther King, Jr.

The year was 1966.

It was a Friday evening, seemingly like the end of most of my fruitful weeks of promoting for Hamm's Brewing Company. I was deep in thought about plans for an upcoming promotional wine and cheese party at a local night club as I pulled up outside the office and turned off the ignition.

I paused for a moment as I gazed at the building that had become like a familiar second home, to reflect and thank God for my amazing good fortune in Houston over the past nine months.

I had rapidly moved up the ladder as a top sale's representative at Hamm's, with the title Promotion Director, and I didn't feel like life could get much better than it already was; I was happy as could be. I stepped out of the company van onto the shiny black asphalt and loosened my tie as I walked towards the beginning of an unexpected new chapter in my journey that I could never have anticipated.

♪♪♪

I opened the door and stepped inside, simultaneously glancing at the bulletin board on the wall in the entryway.

I did a double take.

'How could it possibly be?'

But there was no mistake: There was my name – James Walker – listed among the other people who, as of that moment, were no longer employed. A jumble of feelings and thoughts started spinning in my head.

Some young cats from Minnesota had been recently brought onboard at the Hamm's Brewery business office and they had started letting people go, making those inevitable, yet dreaded, staff cuts. As is so often the case, the last people who had come in were the first to go.

It felt like a rug had been pulled out from under me. What had been a bounce in my step the last time I climbed these stairs to my office, was now what felt like lead in my shoes. I packed up my belongings into what seemed like a very small box in comparison to the vastness of responsibilities and experiences I had been appreciating only a few short hours before.

I trudged down the hall and returned the company credit cards and the keys to the van. Feeling as empty as my former office, I picked up the phone to call my wife, Patsy, to come and pick me up.

Arriving back home, I wanted to wallow in my solitary misery. I pulled out a bottle of Johnnie Walker Red and lay on the living room floor feeling sorry for myself. All the hard work, all that I had built into what I had thought was a valuable role in the company; I had come so far from the days of learning the beer production process.

Or so I had thought.

I was jarred back to my reality when I allowed God, and a glimmer of hope, to enter my heart and mind again.

I heard my mother's voice in my head: "There isn't anything in the world you cannot do if you have patience and perseverance. Don't give up."

My personal pity party was over. I put the half empty bottle away and took a deep breath. I pulled myself together, suddenly determined to make a new start. I called Patsy into the room as I unfolded a map of the United States.

"Honey, see this map," I explained. "What I want you to do is close your eyes and put your hand over the top of it. Wave your hand around and wherever it stops and whatever you point to, that is where we are moving."

2 | Arriving in Five Points

"Only in the darkness can you see the stars."
- **Dr. Martin Luther King, Jr.**

It was a clear night in October when Patsy and I arrived in Denver, with two young kids in tow. It was time to realize a place of opportunity for my long-time vision and goal of owning a radio station, and the chosen location had been up to God, fate, and my faith in Patsy's intuition.

Interstate 70 as a route through Denver was relatively new at the time. The majority of the city portion of the highway had been pretty much completed by 1964. There were still additional finishing touches being put in place as we drove onward in the fall of 1966.

Under a bridge surrounded by construction lights, I stopped the crowded car and small trailer holding all the possessions we were carrying into this new unknown chapter of our lives.

It was 3 a.m. as I reflected on this journey and watched the lights from the planes descending towards Stapleton International Airport. Everyone else was asleep as I awaited the daylight.

♪♪♪

Later that morning, we exited from I-70 onto Federal Boulevard and pulled into a service station to ask for directions to an apartment that would become our first residence on this new venture in the Mile High City.

The first several days were spent moving in and getting settled into our humble abode on Grove Street in West Denver. The weekend arrived. Saturday came and went, and we still had not seen any Black folk. Not even one.

Sunday, Monday, and Tuesday held the same perspective of our new neighborhood. Some serious doubts were beginning to creep into my mind about this supposedly up and coming city of opportunity.

Heavy with skepticism, I said to my wife, "I don't know if this is the right place for us."

After all, my research and inquiry before the move, whether entirely accurate, had indicated that there were approximately 26,000 Blacks in Denver. I was told that much of that population was "a lot of in and out" with the military bases.

Hey, 26,000 was seemingly a market the size of Shreveport, Louisiana, where I spent a good amount of my early years, and a comparison I thought I was familiar with. This number just didn't seem to fit with my current limited experience so far in Colorado.

Midweek rolled around and I walked down Federal Boulevard to Colfax Avenue. I could hardly believe my eyes when I spotted a Black guy driving by me in a car!

I was overjoyed to see him, and I raised my hand in a gesture for him to stop so we could talk. Rather than my anticipated welcoming conversation, the man takes off. I was very puzzled and returned to my wife to relay my most recent experience.

"I really have some serious doubts about this place now. The first brother I see hits the gas," I said, shaking my head in perplexed disappointment.

The next morning, I went back to my trusty reference person at the service station on Federal Boulevard. I asked him if there really were any Black folks here.

He replied, "Yeah, there's Blacks. Take I-70 across I-25 and there's an exit there that's Washington Street."

He proceeded to tell me about this area called Five Points.

My wife and I continued driving on the highway that would soon become as familiar as the back of our hands. We exited onto Washington Street and as we glanced around, I knew, without another question or doubt, we were home.

3 | Early Radio: Path to Houston

"Wisdom does not come overnight."

- Somali Proverb

I graduated from Southern University in Baton Rouge in 1963 with a Bachelor of Arts degree in sociology. Since I couldn't find a really good job in that area of study, both my mother and my sister were encouraging me to obtain a teaching certification. I already knew in my heart I would not be pursuing a formal career in teaching, and I had a dream taking shape in my soul of entering the world of radio.

My first job after college was with an insurance company in Minden, Louisiana, before transferring a few years later to the same company in nearby Shreveport, 45 miles away from my hometown of Gibsland.

As so often happens, God seemed to have a different plan for me than becoming a teacher, or a career insurance agent. My sister was at that time dating a guy in the radio business. He was a so-called "Daddy-O Hot Rod" in Shreveport.

One day while he and I were talking, he began questioning me about what my future plans were going to be. He knew I had a passion for the radio business, and he suggested I do some work with him to determine if radio was something I might be interested in pursuing.

I jumped at this opportunity.

He worked on the air at a radio station with the call letters KOKA, and I found it exciting to watch him do his skilled trade. I soon learned I could use my sociology skills in radio. It was all about communication and dealing with people.

"You're kind of green but I think I could work with you and get you ready for a career in radio," he said to me.

Daddy-O Hot Rod took me under his wing and gave me an opportunity to be in the studio and explore the industry. The manager at the time was looking for someone to work part-time on the weekends. I went on the air Saturdays and Sundays.

I was so excited, and soon discovered that I really wanted a full shift working every day. I began to allow myself to set in motion plans for what could happen next.

I was hearing my mother's voice more and more in my head, "Baby, you can do anything you set your mind to."

I started thinking, 'Maybe I can get into advertising sales.'

In those days, Black individuals weren't allowed to be in sales. We were the announcers and the disc jockeys. But ad sales were, and will always be, where the money is in the radio business.

I found my opportunity to talk with the manager and I asked him about the possibility of pursuing sales.

To my surprise, he said "Ok," and handed me a rate card.

I hit the streets to sell radio advertising time to area businesses. I took my newly acquired quest very seriously, and within the first two weeks I had sold advertising to the largest furniture store in Shreveport. A "Yes" answer from this particular business had been sought by others to no avail ever since the radio station had started.

The people at the station were excited, as well as the manager of the furniture store. I was over the moon that I had made my mark in my corner of the radio industry. I became more and more inspired and as the days and weeks went by, I continued selling new advertisements and making more things happen in my newfound radio advertising world.

♪♪♪

My brother, Charles Walker, was living in Houston at the time. I never had the opportunity to know him very well when I was growing up. He was 24 years older and had moved to Houston when I was 15 years old to start a construction company.

He had been like a father to me in many ways, and Charles was now long married and making his own mark in the construction business.

As fate would have it, Charles entered into a remodeling contract with a radio station owner in Houston. My brother knew I was looking for further radio opportunities and asked the station owner if he was hiring.

"I have a baby brother in Shreveport and he's in the radio business. He's on the air part-time on the weekends and sells advertisements during the week," he proceeded to tell the station owner.

That was an attention-getter since Houston had become a big market with rhythm and blues (R&B) radio stations enjoying popularity throughout the community and gaining momentum across the state of Texas. They had no Black ad salesmen.

"I might be interested," he replied.

After my brother's call to me, I traveled to Houston and struck a deal with this station, KCOH, that held so much promise and possibility. I was filled with gratitude to God for this chance to further advance my radio career and, at the same time, as an added bonus, get to know my brother and build a new family connection.

I wanted to give my two-week notice to the Shreveport station and I was on track for that plan. However, racism reared its ugly head on a day I was expecting a vital phone call from my future employer in Houston.

We were not supposed to take phone calls while we were on the air, and I had adhered to this rule up until this point. I told our secretary, who was also a gospel DJ, that I was expecting a very important call. As luck, or perhaps fate, would have it, not only did I receive the call while on my on-air shift, but the station manager also saw me on the phone as he walked by.

After I hung up the phone upon finalizing details with my new boss in Houston, the owner of KOKA came in the studio and went off on me. His negative and angry overreaction was out of pure ignorance and assumption, and I reacted right back.

"You take this job and stick it," I angrily replied.

He continued to read me the riot act saying, "You'll never get a job in radio!"

"You watch me!" I shot back.

With no more responsibility to stick around for, Patsy and I loaded up a small trailer and headed to Houston. The day after we arrived, I reported to KCOH, telling my surprised new boss that I had changed my mind about the two-week notice.

I never looked back.

4 | Hamm's Brewing Company

"History has shown us that courage can be contagious,

and hope can take on a life of its own."

- Michelle Obama

My time at KCOH marched on, and I felt I had gone as far as I could go on my own in the Houston radio business as a disc jockey. As a DJ, I would do work both inside and outside the station; night clubs, birthday parties, emceeing shows, and working other venues as well.

There were two R&B radio stations in Houston at the time and they were always in competition. Every DJ on the air did beer shows. I landed the opportunity to do the Hamm's beer program and spent about a year and a half doing these big promotions.

The Hamm's Brewing Company began giving me offers to come and work at the brewery in Houston. I finally showed a very appealing contract offer to the radio station owner.

"I can't match it," he said, "but know you can always come back to me."

♪♪♪

Within two weeks of accepting that contract, I had gone through the entire process at the Hamm's Brewery. I knew all about fermentation and filtration. I knew all about beer carbonation. I knew how to bottle. I learned more than I ever imagined there was to know about beer.

After that, I was soon promoted to Promotions Director with all the bells and whistles that could go along with the title. I felt I had found a niche in furthering the vision and exposure of Hamm's, coordinating advertising parties and events at bars, night clubs, restaurants and anywhere beer was sold. I was enjoying my new world of climbing up the corporate ladder and living the company high life.

Nine months later the bottom fell out.

Or so it seemed.

5 | Growing up in Gibsland

"We are the ones we've been waiting for. We are the change that we seek."

- Barack Obama

My mother, Mattie (Ludie) Frazier-Walker, who was born in Ada-Taylor, Louisiana on June 7, 1898, instilled in me a message:

"Son, there is not anything in the world you cannot do. But you've got to have patience. And sometimes, it will take a lot of hard work. And there might be a wait until the time is right. You need to have the time, and the patience."

I grew up a country boy in Gibsland, Louisiana. We had 200 pigs at one point in time. There was a big pasture for the hogs with a large pond for them to wallow in the mud. Since both of my siblings were so much older and had left home, it was just me and my mom taking on all the responsibilities of the farm. My mother was such a strong woman and she single- handedly did so many things to keep everything going.

We also had horses, mules, and chickens. My mother raised everything – all the meat and vegetables – that we ate. About the only items we went to the store for were meal and flour.

I had to get up early and feed the hogs and take care of the horses before I walked for an hour along the railroad tracks to get to school.

At the end of the day, I would walk home, with one main thing on my mind: my mother's cooking.

My mom would butcher the animals herself that we needed for food. There were always chickens running loose in our yard. But the ones she intended to put on the table were in the chicken yard. Mom would also kill four or five hogs at a time.

Always generous and giving, she would fix vast quantities of food from our own natural resources. On Sundays, people would line up after church for pork and collard greens that had been prepared with my mother's abiding love.

Other times, she would fix four or five chickens and have greens, potatoes and all the fixings. She would invite all the surrounding farm neighbors and we would have a community feast.

My mother would bake eight or nine cakes at Christmas and share them with our country neighbors as well. My mom always believed in sharing. We lived in a true community; we helped our neighbors, and our neighbors helped us.

There was always unity in the community.

My mother gave me the nickname, "Buster." Everyone in the community knew me as Buster as I grew up. In fact, if you had arrived in Gibsland for years after and inquired about James Walker, it's likely that no one would have known who you were talking about.

My memories of my childhood on that farm were some of the happiest moments I could ask for.

♪♪♪

My father died of pneumonia two weeks before I was born. The one picture my uncle had of my father was lost in a fire and so I never had an opportunity to see a photograph of the man responsible for my birth. I could only try to imagine and piece together what I thought he may have looked like, or the kind of person he might have been.

My mother and my sister shaped me to be who I am. They were my mentors growing up, and they taught me about real life. My mother was a very strict woman of God and religion was a vital part of who she was.

She believed in education, instilling in me that there is nothing in the world I could not do with a good education.

"You get a good education, and you can be the President of the United States," she would tell me.

I looked at her and thought out loud, "That sure isn't possible."

Dr. Martin Luther King, Jr. came on the scene and my mother shared those same words of opportunity.

I looked at her and said, "That sounds good, but it won't be possible."

Then in November of 2007, Barack Obama was elected president. The following January, two weeks to the day of having back surgery, I climbed in my motor home and traveled to Washington D.C. with my grandchildren for President Obama's historic inauguration. I drove every mile and when I got to the truck stops, I would have to be lifted out of my seat and I was not able to pump my own gas.

But I was determined to be witness to this moment that so many believed they would never see.

It was nine degrees the morning that Barack Hussein Obama II took that sacred oath, and I was there in that bone-chilling cold, warmed by the realization of a dream.

I wouldn't have missed it for the world.

It really was true that the seeming impossible, really was possible. And I could do anything as well. Deep down, I had known that all along.

Mom, you were right.

♪♪♪

My sister, Minnie Walker, was 21 years old when I was born on April 24, 1939, and she was already teaching school. When I was in second grade, her classroom was right across the hall from mine. She was always such an integral part of my life, along with my mother. The two of them were at the head of my world. Since my sister was so much older, people would never assume she was my sister.

Instead, I often would get the question, "How are your mother and grandmother doing?"

After a while, I stopped correcting people on their inquiries. My sister was like a mother to me, so "mother" and "grandmother" it was. I did not need to prove otherwise to anyone. When I was an adult, I would take my actual mother shopping, to appointments, and to church. The perceived roles changed once again: I had so many people ask me if I was her pastor.

Growing up, whenever I asked my mom for something, she would often hesitate. But anything I asked from my sister, she would give me. Looking back, I realize I worked this to my advantage when I was a child the same way children work each of their parents in asking one first, and then the other for a hopeful preferred answer.

Minnie would give me material items such as the best clothing and shoes, as well as the mental and emotional support I needed.

As my sister indulged my wants and needs, I always knew that the most important thing that was being instilled in me was love.

Love was the backbone that became the driving determining principle in my life. Love is at the basis of everything that is healthy and good. Love is what I have been so blessed to receive and to give in so many opportunities in my life.

♪♪♪

I lost my brother in January of 1967, and I lost my mother in August of the same year. For a long time, I was angry.

I asked God repeatedly, "Why would you take both of them from me, so soon and so close together?"

My answer came many years later, in a way I would never have expected. More than a decade after my brother and mother had passed, I was pheasant hunting near Hudson, Colorado with my teenage son, Michael.

I remember vividly we were walking down the railroad tracks and I wistfully said to him, "I wish my mother was here to see my accomplishments."

"Daddy, she is walking with you right now," was my wise son's reply.

I looked at him in quiet awe, and thought to myself, "Wow, he is only 13 years old. Where did he get so much wisdom?"

We continued walking and the voice of a higher power spoke to me very clearly, saying, "I took your mother and your brother so that you could be the man that you are today, and the man that you will continue to become."

After that, I never thought about it anymore. I was at peace and those questions of 'Why?' were gone. I believe in that moment, I truly realized that there is a God, and I have been committed to listening to that voice, that is sometimes subtle and other times very direct, ever since.

I don't follow any other leaders besides God. Close to that Divine Spirit is the wisdom of my mother and sister. These three entities have always been the controlling influences in my life.

My mother and sister opened doors and gave me the opportunity to be who I am today. These two women always were, and continue to be in spirit, my role models; the people who shaped me, the individuals who I look to for guidance, the ones who loved me to the depths of my soul.

When my mother passed, my sister became everything to me. I lost my sister in 2017, at the age of 99. Minnie Walker-Dawson was just two months from turning 100 years old.

6 | Patsy

"If you want to go fast, go alone. If you want to go far, go together."

- African Proverb

On November 29, 2018, the love of my life transitioned to her Kingdom of Glory.

Patsy Ruth Stroman and I fell in love in Gibsland. We experienced our childhoods in the same town, went to the same school, and lived within a half a block of each other growing up. She was 16 years old and I was 18 when our relationship began.

I had graduated from high school and gone to college four hours away at Southern University. One evening when I was on a visit back home, I went over to the high school to watch the girls' basketball game. Pat was a point guard on the varsity team and that evening I was especially impressed with how she played the game.

Afterwards, I asked Pat if I could walk her home. She agreed and we began talking, and from that moment on we just clicked. We started spending time together, and that growing spark soon evolved into doing everything together whenever I was home.

In the beginning, we were just friends, and it was a purely platonic relationship, the kind that builds so much trust and you eventually realize this is the person you want to spend a lifetime with.

When Pat graduated from high school, she went to Grambling College (now Grambling State University) and I continued at Southern, still nearly four hours apart. We were married when she was 19 and a freshman in college. I was 21 and had one year left in Baton Rouge. From that point on, we had the most wonderful life together.

Patsy graduated from college with a degree in business administration. I got a job working with Benevolent Life Insurance, creating new policies and collecting premiums, and holding on tight to my dream of pursuing radio.

Our first daughter, Yolanda, was born when we were living in Shreveport. After we moved to Houston, we were once again blessed; this time with our first son, James, Jr. ("Ricky"). After finding our true home in Denver, two more children were born to our union, Michael and Jasmine.

Pat was supportive and always right there with me through everything, the trials and tribulations as well as the joys and triumphs. I reciprocated with the same strong support in all of her accomplishments and challenges. She was my backbone, and a true partner in every way.

Along with her own endeavors over the years -nursing, teaching and entrepreneurship – she was always right there to help me in any way she could with the radio station, becoming both co-owner and business manager of KDKO. She was my right hand.

Patsy had a true mind and passion for business. In 1969, she opened the very popular Pat's Record Parlor in Denver, which she expanded to five locations across Colorado. During this same time, she also owned Pat's Learning Center, Pat's Transportation Service, and Pat's Tax Service. She was so ambitious and could make magic happen with everything she set her mind to.

My soulmate and partner was an amazing person. I thank God I had a wife who stuck with me. There were good times, and there were some very tough times. There were periods of our marriage that were not easy. In my early days, I was kind of wild and life was fast in the music business. She stayed by my side, even when we reached our most challenging points in our relationship. Through it all, Pat never stopped believing in me and she loved me with the same fierceness that I loved her.

I always tried to be a good provider, as well as supporting her emotionally. I don't think there was anything she wanted that I didn't give her, and I don't think there was a place she wanted to go that she didn't get a chance to visit. I believe there isn't a highway between Denver and Louisiana or Texas that we didn't travel. I don't think we missed out on anything together. We seized life's opportunities as a team.

Pat was always active in church throughout her life, initially Mt. Gilead Baptist Church when we moved to Denver, and then Central Baptist. She taught school in Arizona when we lived there, and later after we returned to Denver, she was teaching in Aurora Public Schools.

I often thought about who would leave this world first. I struggled with her pending loss so much, but now I believe it happened the way it was meant to, because now she no longer has to suffer from illness, and has no more hurt or pain.

We had a great life together. She raised four great kids and was able to nurture and enjoy seven grandchildren and a great grandson in her lifetime. She taught me so many things about life with her exemplary qualities. Patsy was multi-talented and smart, with a quick wit to match. She was committed to everything she was involved in.

Her life can never be forgotten, and she left a lasting impact on everyone she met.

Pat passed two days after our 58th wedding anniversary, we had been together for 60 years. She made it through her birthday and Thanksgiving.

She was a darling. She was a great lady.

And she will always be so missed.

7 | Beginning in Denver and the KDKO Journey

"What you're thinking is what you're becoming."

- Muhammad Ali

The first job I had when I came to Denver was with *The Denver Blade*. A man named Joe Brown was the publisher and owner of this small independent newspaper, and he was one of the sharpest and smartest men I have ever known. He was a promoter, a teacher, and a motivator, and he was very influential in the Black community. He seemed to have control of the city of Denver.

The Blade was an African American weekly paper that was born into existence in 1961 and came off the press every Thursday. Joe Brown had his own printer and his own press. I was there the day the press was installed.

I learned so much from Joe. He was not afraid to write, he was not afraid to fight, and he wasn't afraid to support the Black community. The training I received from this phenomenal publisher has been reflected throughout my life.

Joe Brown believed in thorough education and training of his trade. He had a room filled with nothing but books and tapes. He had an outline set up on how his employees had to go through the entire course. I didn't have a chance to do anything else for a month beyond my 8 to 5 intensive tutorials.

Joe was a Republican and he literally divided the office into a Republican side, with himself and a few others, and a Democrat side where I resided. When he made the decision to run for political office, he put me in charge of the whole advertising department, which I ran for about seven months. I enjoyed the work I was doing, but I was itching to get back into radio.

Joe Brown was a remarkable human being who created an amazing newspaper.

♪♪♪

Along with being a part of *The Denver Blade* when we first settled in Denver, I started working at an Aurora tire store selling tires to everyone who would listen to my warnings of snowy roads and slick tires, and their wives out on the road without good treads. I had become very adept at my sales job and skills as a businessman.

This was only a job for me, a source of income. My dream continued to be to get back into radio and break into the Denver airwaves. I was exploring the well-known radio stations around town, hoping I might be able to get in the door somewhere. But the outcome was always the same – no one was willing to hire someone who looked like me.

Top 40, pop music, and country were king in Denver at the time. A person was hard pressed to find anything else outside of those genres. The only kind of music they played at the tire company was country and western, and I always wore my western gear.

One day, I asked the guy in the neighboring cubicle how many country and western stations were in Denver.

"Two," he replied. "Actually, just one - KLAK," he continued.

"There's another station called KDKO, but they don't have much of a listenership. Actually, it's kind of a joke and other people laugh at them because of the fact they sell commercials for twenty-five cents, a dollar, or whatever they can get."

After our enlightening conversation, I reached for the yellow pages and found KDKO.

When I got home, I told Patsy, "I think I'm going at this the wrong way. I've been trying to start at the top, at KHOW, at KOA, and trying to get in with all these big boys. They're not letting any Blacks enter their realm.

"Maybe I need to start at the bottom," I marveled. "I think I'm going to call this guy at this little-known country station, AM 1510 KDKO, and see what he has to say."

So, I called the station owner and he wanted to meet the next morning. I arrived early and waited in the parking lot. At 8:30 a.m., Dave Segal pulled up in his Jaguar. We sat in conversation in his office until 3 p.m. that afternoon.

Dave Segal had quite a history in radio. Canadian-born, Segal entered the world of broadcasting in 1948. From there, he honed his business skills, owning 15 different radio stations. He purchased the well-known FM station KOSI, the first Top 40 rock station in Denver, before he obtained KDKO.

Mr. Segal was not familiar with what was considered Black radio. It was a whole new concept to him. He had heard of the markets of rhythm and blues music pertaining to Black audiences, but he was a little nervous, and also curious about the sales possibilities.

I promised him I would train the sales staff and teach them the art of selling advertisements in three to four days.

"I'll tell you what," he finally said. "I'm willing to try this. I've got to continue playing country and western from 6 a.m. to 3 p.m. You can do your R&B from 3 p.m. until midnight."

He still wasn't entirely convinced

"How will you get your announcers?" he asked.

"The music will speak for itself," I assured him. "Hopefully, I can get one or two DJs standing by to be here by the beginning of next week."

He took the gamble, and I accepted the challenge. There was a lot of rebellion and repercussions from white listeners at the beginning of this major shift. They were only accustomed to rock 'n roll and country music.

We started playing rhythm and blues on a Friday. That Monday, I went out to Murray Brother's Beer Distributors and met with Paul Murray who owned a number of distribution companies in Denver, six of them serving the Black and Latino communities. There was no promotion or advertising, but the dollars were there, and I knew it.

I sold $68,000 worth of advertising, for all the brands of beer that Murray Brother's was distributing. Coors was out of the question at the time. (Eventually, I ended up selling Coors their first minority advertisement).

I returned to the office and Dave could not believe what had just happened. After that, I was over at Paul Murray's office every day making sure that everyone was happy and there were no problems. Everything seemed to be going along smoothly for two weeks.

Then out of the blue, Paul Murray said, "I have bad news for you. I'm going to have to cancel that contract."

I was completely stunned, and my heart fell to my stomach.

"If your boss doesn't have enough sense to realize what kind of Black market he has with a R&B radio station, I have to withdraw our entire advertising agreement," Paul explained. "I can't support country and rhythm and blues together."

"Would you call and tell him that?" I resolutely asked.

"I damn sure will," he replied.

Paul dialed the phone, and I could visualize Dave reaching to pick up the call in his office at the station. I stood motionless, as a moment later I watched and listened as Paul spoke into the receiver.

"Dave, I love you as a friend and a brother, but if you can't see what you've got, I can't endorse you. My company can't deal with a country and western format happening simultaneously with R&B. It has to be one or the other – your choice on which one – or I have to cancel."

I was certain KDKO would not give up its country and western genre. With a heavy heart, I went to the office early the next morning still in disbelief and feeling hurt about what had transpired the day before.

Dave had arrived before I did.

When I walked in, he said, "Jim, come in and sit down."

I sat down and waited for whatever was going to happen next. Dave picked up the phone and called over to the radio station to talk to Dan Davis, the director. Dan was a hater towards the world of Blacks. Littleton, a predominantly white suburb, seemed to have a high level of blatant racism overall - particularly at that time in the late 60's.

Dave's voice was clear and steady. "Dan, that country song you just played… make that the last country and western record that is ever played on my radio station."

I couldn't hear Dan's response, but I was sure it wasn't good.

Dave slammed the receiver down, turned to me and said, "Now are you happy?"

"You're damn right I am," I replied.

And we never looked back.

♪♪♪

The station known as KDKO arrived on the airwaves in August of 1957. It began with the call letters KMOR in the original Littleton office.

Dave Segal purchased the station from Bob Rubin in 1964, and its call letters were changed to KDKO with a new country and western format. The call letters KDKO originally stood for "Denver's Knock-Out." In 1965, a Platte River flood destroyed the transmitter site, so the studio moved to the building I started in on South Santa Fe Drive in Littleton.

In April of 1967, a new KDKO was born with the slogan "SOUL POWER!" Its birth signified the first radio station in Colorado serving the Black community.

The white community also began to pay attention to this new "soul music." At 4 o'clock every day, I could count on the words of the announcer, "It's SOUL POWER with Dr. Daddio."

That was my cue to say, "It's the good Doctor here, 'specially for you nanny grannies, ya' baby-sitters, midnight ramblers, early morning gamblers, and cop-snitchers, it's the Daddio, live and in living color! The boss with the hot sauce!"

We had our Black Soul DJs: me, Cosmo Harris, Billy Soul, Nite Hawk, Charles Love, and others. We also had our white Soul DJs, including Bob Allen, Don Miller, Sandy Scott, Bill Reynolds, Steve Ross, and that list went on as well. The music we played was by James Brown, The Jackson Five, Gladys Knight and the Pips, The Temptations, The Supremes, and everything Motown.

It wasn't always a smooth and easy transition. It upset a lot of Dave's employees at the time because they were country and western guys through and through, and many of them disappeared.

Within six months, I became the station's operational and general manager; encompassing sales, programming and production. I was also in charge of every training. Over the course of just eight months, KDKO was the number one rhythm and blues station in the country. The community was not just involved with KDKO; KDKO was very involved with the community, particularly the Black community.

Any nonprofit organization could get a public service announcement on the air. And rather than have our DJs read these announcements, we would invite someone from the specific organization to come down to the studio and voice the PSA themselves. Some of these early and young voices included Wellington Webb, Hiawatha Davis, and Cleo Parker Robinson. It was no small feat for people to make that trek to South Santa Fe Drive in Littleton, usually from Northeast Denver.

Not only did listenership grow by leaps and bounds with our soul powered soul radio, our financial gain grew as well. In 1966, the station's annual gross income was $58,000. By 1971, in just five years, that annual number had grown to $250,000. That would translate to considerably more money in today's monetary value.

Dave Segal was once quoted to say, "For the first time in 28 years in broadcasting, I can honestly say my station is serving, rather than prostituting, a group of people. Hell, we're the only identity to 85,000 people. Nobody else is doing anything for them – not in audio, not in video."

Segal continued, "Negro people today are proud. They want to have their own music; they want to identify."

That was right on the mark.

One KDKO listener said "Dave Segal is smart. He knows his radio. It's his station, but we Negros feel like it's ours."

♪♪♪

Our format grew at the station, playing everything from gospel to jazz. At its foundation, the station promoted an ideal that encompassed all listeners with my motto of "Unity in the Community."

The door of opportunity was opened to so many different entertainers during that time. In our early KDKO days, rhythm and blues was one of the fastest growing genres of music, rivaling country and rock and roll. The skyrocketing success of R&B was not due to Black people alone. White audiences were the highest percentage of listeners across the country.

The rating system for radio is called the Arbitron and is similar to the Neilson ratings for TV. The Arbitron ranks radio stations based on the listening preference of a relatively small number of sample homes. And like in television, this exclusive rating system determined how much each station can charge for its advertising time.

With so many stations competing for listeners in each broadcast market, the pressure was on to keep listeners from switching the dial. And Arbitron was a method used to find out what type of music was gaining rising popularity.

All the agencies at that time were white and in control of the money and advertising. The white males owned them, but the media buyers were mainly white women.

The Arbitron surveys were only sent to certain zip codes, and in turn, the predominantly Black Denver zip codes were not included. Our high ratings came primarily from white women. There is no telling where our numbers could have been if the system could have been more inclusive, and the community had its voice.

Country and rock music had been traditionally at the top. We worked hard at KDKO to successfully gain advertising dollars and we generated support across the nation.

8 | Promoting

"If my mind can conceive it and my heart can believe it – then I can achieve it."

- Muhammad Ali

A promoter of a musician is responsible for getting the artist's music played on the radio. When there is enough play on a radio station, more records will be sold and there will be a demand for concerts. It is really all about marketing. It was a great business to be in, and I have so many incredible memories of my time as a promoter.

Back in the day, promoting was more straight-forward than it is now. We didn't have the internet with social media, websites, blogs, or emails. Our main venue for promoting was radio and live performance in the form of concerts or club gigs.

My journey as a promoter started when I was working for the radio station KCOH in Houston. I had a friend working with me at the station who was one of the greatest friends in my life. His name was Lee Frasier- Skipper Lee we called him- and he was a Black millionaire in Houston. He took me under his wing.

Skipper Lee had an early understanding that we could bring entertainers to town and it became a primary source of income for us. As I've mentioned, back in those days you were considered only a disc jockey when you were Black and working at a radio station.

Our independent promoting partnership began to unfold, and every weekend we would put on a concert. Whenever we had an opportunity, we would use the Palladium Ballroom, one of the biggest entertainment centers and facilities in Houston at that time. Once a month, we brought many of the entertainers together by making the concerts a contest for local musicians. At every one of our talent shows, there was a group that called themselves Archie Bell & the Drells. They would win every time.

We started out charging only 75 cents for the show. I was young and inexperienced, so I wasn't yet looking at the bigger picture. I was just focused on the 75 cents, the money that was coming through the door. Seeing beyond that was not one of my main concerns. What Skipper Lee was trying to teach me about the additional piece of promoting went in one ear and out the other.

I still had a lot to learn.

When I truly entered the Black radio market in Denver, I found out I really had to have an understanding of how to promote and how to get the entertainers connected with the listeners.

In those days of vinyl records, the various record labels were easily identifiable in an instant, just by the way they looked. For instance: Atlantic label, red and white; Motown, black and white; and so on. The association of the color alone would automatically register with the mind's eye as to what record company the label belonged to, and in turn the viewer would want to know whose record it was.

One time when I was looking at an Atlantic record, I noticed the artist on the label was Archie Bell & the Drells. As I scanned the entire text, I suddenly stopped reading in amazement. In small print at the bottom, my eye had caught the name Lee Frasier, and it blew me away. I immediately called him up and congratulated him.

I heard the voice on the other end of the receiver reply, "I told you. You didn't hear me, you weren't listening. You have the chance to do the same."

"I know." I replied. "I have the chance to do it all now."

The vision of Lee Frasier's name on the record label was etched in my mind. He had been like a father to me, taking me under his wing in the radio and promoting business. I began to envision my name at the bottom of a label and realized it was now my turn. Here was my chance.

After I saw the Archie Bell & the Drells label with Lee Frasier, I saw what could happen for me in Denver. The first thing I needed to do was to find some local talent that could be promoted under my guidance. A young creative musician, Phillip Bailey, had formed a group with Winston Ford and Dale Hinton called the Soul Brothers. I took them under my wing and became their manager.

Phillip was born and raised in Denver and graduated from East High School in 1969. He was attending college at the time while performing lead vocals. Phillip Bailey always had incredible vocal prowess, range and versatility.

I also began promoting Electric Black, which later became Friends & Love. This R&B band was a larger ensemble with several vocalists including Phillip, as well as Larry Dunn on organ. The band leader was a guy named John Blewin. I really believe we had the greatest group in the city.

After that, I had a group called The Hill Sisters in Los Angeles. There were a couple other groups in the mix over the years that went overseas and had some international acclaim. I can reflect that I had a positive impact on the early musical experience and road to success of all these musicians I at one time managed and promoted, in particular the formation of a band that would become one of the most well-known in the world.

Phillip Bailey was invited to join Earth, Wind & Fire in 1972 by founder and leader Maurice White. Larry Dunn soon followed, as well as another East High grad and talented saxophone player, Andrew Woolfolk. They all moved to Los Angeles and had incredible careers with their renowned combined talent.

Maurice White was a hard-working individual, determined to create one of the finest groups on the planet, and he did just that. Maurice helped bring about the evolution of pop music, mixing it with R&B and jazz, funk and soul, which appealed to a wide variety of audiences.

I was lucky to be a part of their lives. My friend, Perry Jones, became Earth, Wind & Fire's manager. I had the band members on the air at KDKO to talk about their experiences whenever they were in town. I enjoyed watching the growing stars in their new niche and long-term career fame.

Phillip continues to perform with Earth, Wind & Fire, celebrating 50 years of being a lead vocalist. He has been inducted into the Rock and Roll Hall of Fame, the Vocal Group Hall of Fame, and the Songwriter's Hall of Fame.

♪♪♪

A couple years after I started working at KDKO, I formed a promoting partnership with a man by the name of Paul Mack.

Our relationship began like spontaneous combustion. Paul had started his promoting career when he was in college at Berkeley. The first act he brought to the West Coast was Donny Hathaway, and from there his journey took off and led him to me.

Paul had done quite a bit of promoting in California by that time, and he decided he wanted to expand his efforts to Denver. He reached out to me out of the blue one day in 1971. Having looked up R&B radio stations in Denver, Paul picked up the phone, called KDKO, and asked to speak to the program director.

"This is The Daddio. What can I do for you?"

"Hey, my name is Paul Mack, and I'm a concert promoter," I heard the voice on the other end say.

"What you talkin' about?" was my reply.

"Look I have these artists who are telling me they want to expand more dates and concert locales. Are you interested?"

"Absolutely,"

It was an easy answer.

From that point on, we just clicked.

Around that time The Dramatics had a number one song called "In the Rain" (1971). Funkadelic had a hit song called "Loose Booty" (1972). The Spinners had their classic, "Could It Be I'm Falling in Love" (1972). Donny Hathaway released "Someday We'll All Be Free" (1973).

Back then, the musicians had true class, style and real talent, performing on stage in their sharp, colorful suits. In a classic R&B band there was usually a piano or keyboard, at least one guitar, bass, drums, saxophone, lead vocalist(s) and sometimes background vocals. It was a unique musical era. The lyrical themes expressed the spectrum of emotions and the Black experience of joy and pain, triumph and tribulation, and the pursuit of freedom.

Paul Mack and I agreed on a title for our newfound promoting business, combining our names into JMack Presents. The magic began to unfold, and he and I began bringing in numerous musicians; The Dramatics, Funkadelic, Tower of Power, Donny Hathaway, War, The Spinners, the Ohio Players, and others. For many of these groups, it was the first time they had performed in Denver, so it was groundbreaking.

I had secured East and Manual high schools as our designated venues, and I put up all the advertising through KDKO and other connections. Our audiences were in the range of 1000 to 1500 people. One of our most distinct memories was counting money on the bathroom floor of the school after our first show.

Everybody was happy. The artists always got paid, and we made money. We did well on our efforts. We expanded our promoting outside of Denver and travelled around successfully bringing concerts to about eight major cities, as far east as Ohio.

For one of our Ohio concerts, we secured Donny Hathaway and Bobby Womack for a show in Columbus. We didn't know it at the time, but Donny was dealing with some emotional issues. He missed the date and didn't show up for the concert. Bobby still performed but since Donny was supposed to be headlining, we had some pretty unhappy fans, and we almost had a riot on our hands.

Paul stayed in the fray and waited for the sheriff to arrive. He was trying to defend our position and was pretty fired up. As a result, he ended up in jail that night. I had to make a move so both of us wouldn't be locked up. I arranged for the needed refunds, made my escape, and then bailed out Paul.

The next day, we went to the bank to divvy up the funds to give to the ticket holders. We really had to scramble to refund it all. We got a bank draft and transferred money to the county treasurer to reimburse the patrons' purchase.

Paul and I got out of town quickly after that. That turned out to be one of the most memorable shows we did together.

Our joint promoting journey had its challenges, as we had to compete with Barry Fey and other great concert promoters around the country. But we had a unique element to our blooming business partnership – we were Black. We were able to make all the connections in the exploding genre of rhythm and blues music.

During that time, Paul and I became like brothers. After a while, we were beginning to envision spreading our wings individually, and our partnership evolved to a natural close. Paul Mack and I had an amazing partnership for about a year and a half.

When we went our separate ways professionally, we continued our respective promotion ventures. Paul Mack is still promoting in California today, primarily gospel. We remain close friends and stay in regular contact.

♪♪♪

Around 1973, I began bringing concerts to Denver on my own. Initially I had been bringing in some lesser-known musicians, and I was experiencing a great deal of frustration that I wasn't able to get into night clubs for the shows I wanted to promote. The groups weren't big stars for the big arenas.

As had become my pattern throughout my life, I turned my anger into finding a solution to my problem.

Wayne Hightower and Jimmy Best owned the club 23rd Street East. They were experiencing some infighting, so I decided to buy the club from them. I named the spot, Daddio's Showcase of Stars. Eventually I franchised and opened a club by the same name in Colorado Spring. I would play the stars in Denver on Friday, and in the Springs on Saturday, or vice versa.

In addition to a guaranteed place to bring entertainment to the community, Daddio's Showcase of Stars also became the site for concert after-parties. The clubs remained active and in existence for almost five years.

During that time, the names were getting bigger in my expanding involvement in the industry. I brought The Jackson 5 and Lionel Richie to the same stage on the same show. My daughter, Yolanda, introduced Michael Jackson onto the stage.

I got the promoting fever, and I put my passion, know-how and growing experience into building relationships with entertainers all over the country. I quickly learned that relationship is what is at the foundation. It was, and still is, what promoting is about.

I was able to do some degree of promoting when I became

established working at KDKO. During this era, it had to remain more of a side gig. However, after I purchased the station, I was able to spend more time and energy with my promoting passion and truly allow it to be a focus. I had more freedom being the station owner, and the boundaries were less limiting.

It was a fulfilling feeling to bring talented Black artists to entertain the community, and in turn, to create opportunities for the musicians.

Promoting has benefits for all who are involved; it is certainly not a one-way street. The entertainers were instrumental in giving the opportunity to radio stations to play their music. Musicians and groups gave me the opportunity to bring them to Denver.

The field of promoting had its share of extra challenges due to the institutional racism that prevailed in the industry. A Black music promoter who had close personal connections to the rhythm & blues artists was threatening to the status quo.

Along with the ups and downs, the memories and the stories that I gained over the years through promotion were so amazing and inspiring. It was a three-way gift; to the community, to the performers, and to me.

It was yet another of God's examples of inter-connectedness, unity and oneness.

♪♪♪

While I was working in Houston, I would premiere many records on the air; what we called "breaking the record." I was honored to have the opportunity to get to know James Brown through this process. I thought very highly of him both as a musician and a man, and over time, he and I became like brothers. After I came to Denver, I was able to give him his first appearance in the Mile High City.

James always booked his own concerts. He didn't have an outside promoter; he was a promoter. King Records was his label, and he put out star after star, besides himself.

He called me up one day shortly after I had started at KDKO and said, "I understand you have a Black radio station in Denver now."

I described KDKO and he continued, "Look man, I have been trying to get into Denver for I don't know how long. They won't give me the facility. Now I can at least have my music played on the air since KDKO is there."

I knew I wanted to be able to do better than merely playing his records; and there had to be a way he could perform live in Denver. We agreed to both keep thinking about it. After all, where there's a will, there is always a way.

Not long after, I picked up the phone and heard James Brown's voice on the other end of the line, "I'm doing a concert in Omaha. Can you meet me there?"

We talked backstage in Omaha. James said he had thought of an idea, and he asked if I could run a commercial about not being "allowed" to perform at the main venues in Denver. I ran two commercials on KDKO in collaboration with his team. It wasn't too long before I received a call from James.

"You can stop running the ads. They gave me the city."

That was the power of radio when it was a main source of media and a primary place where people received information. There was a lot of influence across all races and walks of life. James would call me at KDKO to request bookings in the city, and every time he came to town he was guaranteed to perform.

He became increasingly more significant in both my life and to Colorado. James Brown was not only the "Godfather of Music," he was also the Godfather to my youngest son, Michael.

I brought him on my radio program every opportunity I had whenever he would be in Denver to perform. I have memories of walking with him along Welton Street discussing the development of Five Points, when gentrification of the neighborhood was continuing its onward march.

In 1993, the Chamber of Commerce in Steamboat Springs conducted a poll of its residents to choose a new name for the bridge that crosses the Yampa River on Shield Drive. The winning name, with 7,717 votes, was *James Brown Soul Center of the Universe Bridge*.

The bridge was officially dedicated in September of 1993, and James appeared at the ribbon-cutting ceremony. Busloads of people from Denver and all over the state travelled up to the mountains for its dedication.

James Brown stepped out of the limousine dressed in an electric blue jumpsuit and a dark blue neckerchief. He sang his classic song, "I Feel Good" to an electrified crowd. That night, "The Hardest Working Man in Show Business" hosted a benefit concert. He returned to Steamboat Springs July 4, 2002, to perform at another festival.

In 2006, before James Brown died at the age of 73, a petition was started by a group of residents to return the name to its original title of *Stockbridge* for historical reasons. In their opinion, the name was more aligned with the mountain community's traditional ranching roots. This dissenting group backed off after both the City Council and supportive citizens defeated their efforts. Although still controversial, the name of the bridge remains.

James Brown was one of the most deserving people I know to have a bridge named in his honor.

♪♪♪

I had many incredible opportunities to meet musicians from across the country when I brought them to Denver. And it was so important to me to provide opportunities for the community to interact, and be directly involved, with the various entertainers when they came to town to perform.

Gladys Knight and the Pips were among the numerous artists who I would invite to my house for barbeques and fish fries. There was a park across the street from my home where we would play softball games with people in the community so they could also know the amazing talent offstage as well.

I'll never forget when Gladys Knight gave me the ultimate compliment. "Daddio, why don't you open a restaurant? Your food is so good!"

I told her that I wasn't interested in doing cooking outside my own backyard at that point in time. However, her flattering words stayed in my mind to influence my future endeavors.

We celebrated B.B. King's 50th birthday in 1975 at Daddio's Showcase of Stars. It was a memorable $10,000 event: the after-party following his concert at the Coliseum on a Sunday night.

When the police arrived to try and break up the party and charge us with selling alcohol after midnight, I could truthfully tell them that all the liquor was free and it was being given away so we were not breaking any legal ordinance. The late City Councilman Elvin Caldwell was there, along with the mayor of Denver at the time, William H McNichols, Jr. And since the police chief Art Deal was enjoying himself as an invited guest, the festivities continued until 6 a.m.

At that time, the Denver Coliseum was the only venue where we were bringing big name acts. One of the greatest concert experiences I had in my lifetime was when we brought in The Temptations and had them perform in the middle of the floor, with the audience on all sides of them.

At the conclusion of their performance, it took two and a half hours to move them off the stage, in part due to the primarily female fans who would not leave. We were not able to break down the stage into the crowd. It took some proactive encouragement, and mostly patience, to accomplish the task.

One of my proudest moments was when I created the opportunity to have Gladys Knight and the Pips, along with Smokey Robinson and the Miracles, on the stage together for an unforgettable concert experience.

I went from promoting rhythm and blues to promoting new generations and genres of music, and that continued until I sold KDKO in 2002. Blues became a true niche of my promoting, starting with JMack Presents. B.B. King, Bobby Bland, and Little Milton were a few of these amazing artists. Arzell J. Hill, also known as Z.Z. Hill, was credited with helping to restore the blues to Black consciousness. His track, "Down Home Blues" (1982), has been called the best-known blues song of the 1980s.

I had Z.Z. Hill booked to appear in concert at the beginning of May in 1984. On April 27, just days before he was scheduled to perform in Denver, he died from a heart attack caused by a blood clot that formed after being involved in a car crash two months prior. He was only 48 years old.

That was one of the most heartbreaking and disappointing moments of my promotions career. It was such a loss to have a talented life cut so short.

♪♪♪

Over time, the venues for performances I was able to promote continued to increase. I was able to bring in big name musical artists to the Colorado Black Arts Festival, Juneteenth, and other community events.

The Colorado Black Arts Festival was created in 1986 as a venue for Black visual artists and performers to have an opportunity to display and demonstrate their work and talent. This Denver annual weekend outdoor festival in July has become an important artistic and cultural event that draws artisans from all over the world.

Juneteenth marks the anniversary proclaiming freedom for enslaved African Americans in Texas, and the rest of the United States. The official announcement of this federal enforcement was made by U.S. Army troops arriving in Galveston Bay, Texas, on June 19, 1865.

Contrary to popular belief, the Emancipation Proclamation, issued by President Abraham Lincoln during the Civil War on January 1, 1863, did not free all enslaved people in the United States. It applied to only the ten southern states that were in rebellion at that time, so did not cover the nearly 500,000 other individuals enslaved in Missouri, Kentucky, Maryland, and Delaware. Texas was the last state in the confederacy to gain its freedom due to slaveholder obstruction. For this reason, Juneteenth is a vital holiday to recognize the true "end" of slavery.

Juneteenth was a celebration that I grew up with in Louisiana. From the time I can remember, my family and my community observed and valued June 19. When I was young, we celebrated the declared end of slavery wherever we were, at home, in church, and out in the community. Juneteenth was not a commercialized holiday; it truly meant something. We commemorated Emancipation Day through uniting community activities: baseball, softball, picnicking. Everything was free. It wasn't a way to make money.

When I came to Denver, it was the Richardson brothers who had recently started coordinating the Denver Juneteenth celebration. Otha Rice, Sr. a prominent Black business owner in Five Points originated Colorado's Juneteenth festivities in the early 1950's after arriving in Denver from Texas, with the first official Denver Juneteenth Festival in 1966.

As with so many aspects of my life, my involvement with the Denver Juneteenth celebration started through KDKO, advertising, publicizing and interviewing people connected with the events.

I was soon in charge of coordinating Juneteenth after KDKO became a sponsor. I continued to organize the annual event throughout my time at the station up until selling 1510. For me, it was never just another summer festival. The holiday signifies community barbeques, community service and self-improvement.

I thought the Juneteenth celebration had come into its lasting prime after I purchased KDKO and was able to move both the station and Juneteenth into the Five Points neighborhood. However, after light rail arrived on Welton Street in the mid-nineties, it became an obstacle at that time to the celebration. I knew they weren't going to stop the rail from running for the day, which could be a safety hazard for a festival with so much foot traffic.

In addition, around that same time there was a great deal of media attention to gang violence in the neighborhood. The coverage was blown out of proportion to the reality, and major sponsors of the event began pulling out due to their fears of crime and image.

I was seeing the handwriting on the wall of the impact all of this would have on the Juneteenth holiday, along with so many other shifts happening in Five Points. I made the decision to move the annual celebration to the Montbello neighborhood in Denver.

I chose an undeveloped field for the festival location. Seeing a guy with a big grass cutting machine on the back of his truck driving down I-70, I flagged him down to ask if I could hire him to cut the long grass and weeds in that vacant lot. He told me he was on his way to give a demonstration of the machine, but he could mow for me on his way back. The space was transformed and ready for the event.

Unfortunately, there was a lot of controversy from people who were resistant to the location change. It turned into a lot of infighting and backstabbing among these powers that be towards me and my choices. I ultimately had to discontinue the Juneteenth festival after about four or five years at Montbello. We were out of options at the time and so Denver's official celebration had to be put on hold for a few years.

Norman Harris III, grandson of the late Norman Harris, Sr. of Five Points, has brought the Juneteenth celebration back to life again. Now called the Juneteenth Music Festival since 2012, its musician line-ups are scheduled at several different performance stages, as well as the traditional parade and vendor opportunities along Welton Street once again.

9 | Tucson

"Smooth seas do not make skillful sailors."

- African Proverb

In 1980, Dave Segal sold KDKO to Sterling Broadcasters, and the new owners moved the studio to South Denver into an area referred to as the Denver Tech Center. Before this happened, I knew it was time to step away, at least temporarily, as I was experiencing increasing conflicts with Dave.

The day I left KDKO, I said to Dave Segal, "I will own KDKO one day."

In the meantime, I had an opportunity to go in with a couple of other guys in the radio business who were looking to buy a station in Tucson, Arizona. My broker, Ray Hambric, was working on both sales, KDKO and the radio station in Tucson. Since my KDKO purchase appeared to be at a standstill, Ray suggested that I go ahead and collaborate with these guys who were focused on a rock 'n roll genre. I agreed, and Pat and I, along with our young daughter, Jasmine, packed up the moving van to begin our Arizona chapter.

We had both the AM and FM frequencies; KFOX were the FM call letters and KKPW were the AM. I programmed on the AM with my rhythm and blues, and they programmed the FM with their rock. We successfully got both parts of the station off the ground and running smoothly, operating together at the same facility with our respective musics.

My community involvement in Tucson was similar to what it was in Denver, including live broadcasts at shopping centers and other businesses. The station was in charge of planning the first St. Patrick's Day celebration. That was memorable for me and for everyone else, a Black man coordinated the parade and the other Irish holiday events.

My overall experience living in Tucson was also similar in many ways to what it was in Denver. I adjusted to the weather patterns, and the heat. I figured out if you can make it from May to October, you had it made. After the sizzling summer, the weather was ideal.

Once again, just like KDKO in the Mile High City, the station became the voice for the Tucson Black community promoting change and making things happen. I dealt with the same issues that I did in Denver, except Tucson was a much smaller community.

The racial climate was very different in Tucson because there were comparatively few Blacks living there. It was an interesting phenomenon. At first, it appeared that there was a great deal more acceptance and racial progressiveness in the white population of Tucson and Arizona as a whole. However, over time, it became apparent that the illusion of this attitude seemed to be attributed to the actual lack of diversity and, in turn, the non-threat of a loss of white power. The numbers of African Americans at that time were not high enough to pose any type of perceived threat.

A couple stations in Phoenix started playing R&B music. There wasn't competition between us because we had two different geographic markets.

The station support from the Tucson community was obvious. When the Albritron ratings came in, it was like what had happened in Denver. The majority of positive ratings went towards the R&B music, once again from white listeners.

As had been the case in Denver, it wasn't the Black community in Tucson that supported the station and carried us. It was the white community. They voted for us, since they were the ones who were selected to participate in the ratings. The support for Black music transcended race. This was rewarding and encouraging for me. I really wanted to trade the AM for the FM, and it only made sense to me since the R&B was where the ratings were concentrated.

"Y'all take the AM for the rock and let me take the FM for the rhythm and blues," I proposed to them after my careful analysis and consideration.

But they didn't want to do that. It all felt somewhat confusing to me.

I said "Ok," and went along with it.

After that, there was some negativity on both sides, and it impacted our working relationship and attitude towards one another. It probably was all part of the signs that Denver is where I knew I really wanted to be, and where I felt I belonged.

When I left both Louisiana and Houston, I had originally thought about going to Arizona. Something about it made it an enticing location to me. After my wife's hand landed on Denver on the map, I had the back-up option that if that didn't work out, we could go from there to Arizona.

The grand plan of life gave us a chance to experience both Denver and Arizona. God brought those wants and desires together for me after all. My two primary goals of places to make a mark for myself and experience the locations to the fullest; I was able to accomplish them both.

Patsy, Jasmine and I stayed in Tucson for about three and a half years while I was co-operating the station, and we became well established in the community. I was involved in many civic and social organizations, including the National Association for the Advancement of Colored People (NAACP) and the Urban League. My wife found a niche in the elementary school system, and other areas. Our time in Arizona was a happy and fulfilling time for both me and Patsy.

♪♪♪

I was staying connected with KDKO, the station that was so much a part of my heart and soul. When I was ready to put my car in the garage at my home in Tucson, I could listen to KDKO as I could pick up the signal at that spot at night. I would sometimes sit there for an hour or more to gain as much as I could about what was happening at the station.

Denver radio sportscaster Thierry Smith would keep me updated on what was happening back in Denver as well. Thierry had graduated from East High School in the early 70s and went on to achieve a degree in communications from the University of Denver.

He had started out as a cub reporter at KDKO, where he evolved to host a midday "Sports Rap" show at the station. Later, he moved over to KYBG and KKFN where he worked both the AM and FM dial. Eventually, he ended up at FM 104.3 KKFN "The Fan."

For years, Thierry was the only Black voice in the crowded Denver sports talk show business. In 2000, he was given a well-deserved Lifetime Achievement Award from the Colorado Association of Black Journalists.

One day, he called me.

"Doc, I heard KDKO is for sale."

My heart skipped a beat, and I immediately dialed Ray, my broker in Denver, to get more details about the situation.

I flew from Tucson to Los Angeles to talk with Fred Danz, who was then the owner of KDKO and about nine other stations, along with some bowling alleys, around the country. He had bought the station from Dave in 1980. Fred was in the entertainment business, and I knew he didn't have a personal investment, or interest, in KDKO so it was worth a shot.

After listening to my proposal, Fred replied, "Yeah, if you get the money together, we can discuss this further."

"I got the money," I said, trying to temper the height of my excitement.

I had been working hard with some other investors to create this moment.

"Ok, let's get together on a price and make it happen," were Fred's welcome words. It felt like music to my ears.

That was on a Friday evening. On Monday, I met with my attorney in Denver to start drawing up the paperwork. There was a bounce in my step. We had a deal on the table. The plan was that after we sold the stations in Tucson, I would be the owner of KDKO. Apparently, it was not meant to be that easy.

When I returned to Denver, Adams Communication, the people buying the other radio stations currently belonging to Mr. Danz decided they needed to buy them all in a package. They were very firm that they would only separate it for a ridiculous price.

I begrudgingly had to say, "No, that's not going to work."

I was very disappointed and felt like my dream had a real setback, but once again, I was not going to give up on my long-term vision I had already worked so hard to realize and invested so much of my soul.

It also seemed obvious to me that the community wasn't quite ready for a Black radio station owner, and a very outspoken one at that.

After nearly four years in Arizona, Patsy and I decided it was time to close the window of that great experience and open the door for being able to fight for the community and do my part to help the future of the city of Denver. It was ever more apparent that was what God wanted me to do.

10 | KDKO Ownership

"The best way to make your dreams come true is to wake up."

- Muhammad Ali

About four months after returning to Denver from Tucson, there was a radio broker convention in Washington D.C. This financial conference was important to my latest plan - I was ready to pursue and solicit another financial supporter as an investor. My determination was not to be deterred.

The time of the conference rolled around, and I was at the D.C. hotel enjoying breakfast with a Black guy who had owned the well-known WLAC radio station in Nashville. He had recently sold his radio station and was now a Federal Communications Commission (FCC) attorney in Washington D.C.

A man walks up to our table and shakes hands with my meal companion. I casually noticed his nametag read "Adams Communication."

Instinctively, I reached out my hand to him and said, "Well, congratulations."

"Congratulations for what?" he asked.

"You bought a station in Colorado, KDKO in Denver," was my reply. "I also recently heard that you pulled out the Seattle station and made a deal with someone else."

I had been doing due diligence in my research after the fallout and tracking any changes. I inquired what they were planning to do with KDKO since they had already separated the stations they had originally been so adamant about keeping together.

I saw recognition register on his face as he realized who he was talking with.

"I understand you had your package together and were all set for a purchase," he said with seeming interest.

He listened intently as I proceeded to share those past painful details and then he said, "Let me call the office and by noon I should have an answer for you."

He invited me to meet him back at the hotel for lunch later. I was so excited. I could hardly wait. My adrenaline began to pump again, and I rushed back to the hotel to call Pat.

"I don't dare speak too soon, but it really looks like things might be on track again!"

And luckily, they were.

Mr. Adams Communication arrived for lunch with a wide smile on his face as he exclaimed, "Jim, I think we have a deal."

I immediately returned to my room to pack and boarded a plane back to Denver where Pat was waiting for me. Our minds, our hearts, and our souls were filled with the excited anticipation for the next chapter in our ongoing journey.

KDKO was finally actually ours. It was time to be back home in Denver for good.

One of the greatest highlights and happiest moments of my life was the day in 1989 I closed on the ownership of KDKO with our company, People's Wireless, Inc. Ray Hambric and I put together a business plan for KDKO and applied for some available money from the Denver Economic Development & Opportunity office under Mayor Federico Pena. In order to receive the funding, I had to explain how KDKO would give employment to minorities, which was easy for me to demonstrate. With capitol from the city and my investors, our long-awaited dream finally became a reality.

A major thrill of purchasing KDKO was moving the station to Five Points. This was a part of my dream for the station, to be in the heart and the hub of the history of where the Denver Black community began.

Every day was something different. Each day presented a new challenge. We had our highs and lows spanning the 13 years of ownership, from 1989 to 2002. During that decade plus, I was able to be involved in so many facets, from operations to promotions to Daddio's Kitchen on Wheels. Looking back, I don't know how there were enough hours in each day.

I became known at KDKO as the "Blues Man." My operation was more with the blues than Top 40. I played more blues than average, and most of the shows I was bringing to town at that time evolved to be mostly of the blues genre. Most of the music I played was from artists like B.B. King, Bobby Bland, Johnnie Taylor, Little Milton, and the list went on. I mixed in Motown; The Temptations, Gladys Knight, Smokey Robinson, The Supremes, among many others.

It was a wonderful balance that took on a life of its own, with its rhythm and flow.

I worked with many memorable people at KDKO. During my

time as owner, I had several different program directors. I gave Kevin Brown his first job as manager of KDKO. Kevin had a disco business in New York and had also been involved in radio. He had come out to Colorado to go to law school at Denver University, but he didn't have enough money for the following semester, so he came to KDKO inquiring after a job.

I told Kevin we needed commercials created. He assured me he could handle any equipment and produce the commercials I was looking for. Less than an hour later, there was a knock on my office door and Kevin informed me the initial commercials I asked for were complete.

"You've got a job," I said.

At that time, we held a lot of station parties and contests at a restaurant in Denver called Baby Doe's. One evening we were on the patio having a holiday company barbeque. It was snowing.

A man in his early 20s approached my table and said to me, "Daddio, you are an outstanding man. I really appreciate your vision."

Terry Hutt was a Denver native working on the air at KDKO, but I hadn't talked with him extensively. As our conversation continued, I recognized that our visions were similar, and I knew right away we would work well together. I hired him as my program director, and I never regretted it. He did a fantastic job.

Terry wasn't married at the time he was working with me. After I had sold KDKO, I was at the grand opening of the Boys and Girls Club when I felt someone touch me on the shoulder. I turned around and it was Terry.

He told me that he was there with his young daughter. I couldn't believe that he was married and had both a daughter and a son. It was always amazing to watch people change and grow.

It was so fulfilling to be able to be influential in advancing the growth of businesses in the community, particularly Black enterprise. Car dealers, banks, restaurants, retail, and any other business you could think of thrived at that time, in part I like to believe because my ability and venue of endorsement and promotion contributed to the community's entrepreneurial success. KDKO was also instrumental in building awareness around Black churches, helping to pack their Sunday services.

On the fifth anniversary of my ownership of KDKO, I brought Dave Segal from the audience onto the stage at our celebration at the Holiday Inn at I-70 and Chambers, now the Crowne Plaza Hotel, to acknowledge his role in my journey.

When Dave had the microphone, he surprised me with his speech.

He turned to me and said, "Nobody has ever given you anything. You deserve to own KDKO because you have worked for it."

That was a moment that will always stay with me. I had waited a long time to hear those words from him. He finally acknowledged my perseverance and diligence.

Even though he and I had experienced a rocky relationship at times over the years, it was a humbling experience from a man that I owe a great deal of my Denver radio success. Without the opportunity Dave provided me to guide the path of the KDKO rhythm and blues journey, I may not have been where I was in the realization of my long-term dream.

Dave Segal passed away in 2013. He was 80 years old.

♪♪♪

I felt like I was a threat to many people in the radio business. I was not a quiet Black man who was satisfied with the status quo. I needed to be the voice for the Black community, for people who were often not heard. That was my self-designated role.

My efforts to create change and equality were at times met with resistance and racism. Plus, the traditionally white radio owners did not want to see a Black man rising in their ranks.

As I said earlier, the Denver zip codes that were considered to be in "Black neighborhoods" did not receive the Arbitron rating booklet throughout the time I was with KDKO. And fortunately, that still worked out since we had a cross-over white population who appreciated rhythm and blues music.

In funding however, KDKO ended up with the crumbs on the table. KOA and the other major white-owned radio stations always seemed to end up with the big bucks in the pot. The sponsorship money was now required to be primarily corporate in order to compete, rather than also from independent businesses as in the past.

I could get corporate advertisers such as Coors, Coca-Cola, and Pepsi. However, everyone was experiencing budget cuts in the early 2000s following 9/11 and the stock market crash. The generous amounts that I could obtain in the beginning, and for many years, were no longer being offered – especially to a Black-owned independent business. I could no longer get the revenue that was needed for my operation.

The support was not there like it had been in previous years. The doors were beginning to close. The advertisers weren't coming in. The only way to operate was through national and local advertising revenue and those dollars were easing out of the market.

Billions of dollars of advertising went to Jacor Communicatons, Inc., one of the nation's largest operators of radio stations. It felt like we were getting just nickels and dimes, and it seemed to be happening to stations, and other independent businesses, all over the country.

I was seeing the future for Black radio.

Berry Gordy sold Motown Records to MCA in 1988 for $61 million, after 28 years of developing, creating and growing his vision and realized dream of the Motown entitiy. I could connect strongly with his decision and his reasons. Berry felt that he could no longer compete with the much larger, non-independent companies.

Berry had thrived while crossing racial barriers in the music industry, but he broke these barriers at the price of sacrificing most elements of Blackness. Berry did not want to limit himself to Black radio stations or the Black touring circuit. He felt the only way he could get white radio stations to play Motown was to hire an all-white sales and marketing team. He believed that selling music had to be done in a non-threatening way so Black faces did not appear on the first few albums of Motown.

Berry learned the harsh reality of selling to a white audience at a young age. As a child, he made money by selling the *Michigan Chronicle*. He started out selling the paper in Black neighborhoods, but soon discovered he could make more cash by selling to white customers as well.

That is until he brought his brother with him to sell newspapers, and suddenly he realized that one Black kid was seen as cute, but two were perceived as a threat. This time, no one spoke to him, and zero papers were sold.

In Berry Gordy's autobiography, *To Be Loved,* he tells the story of Jesse Jackson telling him that "selling Motown would be a blow to Black people all over the world."

Berry's reply was, "I have three choices – sell out, bail out or fall out."

There were some echoes in that for how I was feeling a decade after. I was becoming disenchanted with the industry of both radio and promotions. The changing business climate, nationwide, had become no longer a good fit for either one of us over the years, or for many old-school independent businesspeople, particularly minorities.

There were, and still continue to be, many forms of economic control of the Black businessperson. The bottom line is that if you don't get the revenue, you can't operate. That was the main reason why I sold the station; it was time to make the move and get out.

In addition, it became increasingly more difficult for a sole owner of any race to be able to maintain a profitable radio station. By the turn of the 21st century, the times were rapidly shifting, and it was common for the big conglomerates to have eight stations under one roof. This made it nearly impossible to have the needed ratings and support for a single independently owned radio station.

Denver's only Black Soul Station ended its broadcasting days in May of 2002. Denver Billionaire Phillip Anschutz, with Newspaper Radio Corporation, bought the station. KDKO became KRNC, changing its format to news talk radio on June 24, 2002, and moving to its new downtown studios.

KRNC only lasted for two years. The station met its final demise in 2004.

After selling KDKO my wife and I travelled for about six months. We had bought an RV and we drove all around the country. Yolanda ran the three separate Daddio Kitchen on Wheels restaurants while we enjoyed our much-needed break and cross-country adventures.

11 | Daddio's Kitchen on Wheels

‖‖‖‖‖ 🎤 ‖‖‖‖‖

"You must never be fearful of what you are doing when it is right."

- Rosa Parks

After purchasing KDKO and moving it to Welton Street in Five Points, I was pondering what could be an additional business draw at the radio station's new location, something that would attract the diverse population of northeast Denver in the already rapidly changing neighborhood, primarily due to gentrification.

It was the early nineties, and the Regional Transportation District (RTD) was just on the brink of bringing their Metro Area Connection (MAC) light rail to Denver, which would add a whole new dimension of possibilities. With promise of further access through another form of public transportation, the light rail was being built along Welton Street and would travel many times daily from downtown through the heart of Five Points.

I needed to create something that could be a draw, not only for the surrounding residents and workers, but also for the light rail patrons that would be passing through. After much thought, research, and reflection, I came to the strong conclusion that "something" should be surrounding cooking.

In the back of my mind, I could hear Gladys Knight's voice asking me, "Daddio, why don't you open a restaurant?"

I was finally ready to change my answer.

♪♪♪

On a trip home for my family reunion in Louisiana, I stumbled across just what I was looking for. It was what I had envisioned.

There were people attending this reunion from all over the country and our main gathering was being held in a large event center. As I drove into the parking lot with my sister, I caught sight of a guy on the back of a 20-foot trailer wearing a white uniform and a white chef's hat working over a smoker and barbeque grill. There was a very nice truck attached to this beautiful trailer.

I said out loud, "Wow, that's what I want, the ability to smoke meat and serve the best barbeque to large masses of hungry people!"

I parked nearby and walked over to this man who was about to help another dream of mine become a reality. It was an experience that, like so many God has revealed to me, was filled with life connections, much fewer than the classic six degrees of separation.

I found out later the man busy cooking on the trailer was a school principal who knew my sister. In fact, he had previously worked at the same school where she had been a teacher.

What a small world.

When I inquired about his rig, he explained to me that he had seven barbeque units. He gave me his phone number and a few days later I called and left him a message. I was so determined to talk with him before I had to leave to head back to Denver that I decided I would make a trip over to the school where he currently worked.

Once again, God was at work in my life. I inquired after him in the main office, and he had some time to talk with me. We took a walk and proceeded to have a more in-depth conversation on the possibility of striking up a deal on a purchase of a smoker.

We ended up in the school parking lot and I saw him glancing at the front of my car. He confessed to me that he initially thought I lived locally, and he had been somewhat purposely avoiding me since he was feeling uncomfortable about having any competition in the area.

He said rather sheepishly, "Now that I've learned from your license plate that you're from Colorado, I would be happy to sell you one to take back to Denver."

The next day, my new friend took me to see another fellow in Grambling, Mr. Walden, who built the smokers. We all ended up being very close. Mr. Walden built the initial one for me to take back to Colorado, followed by my second smoker at a later date.

Over the course of time, I had three ten-foot trailer units built by a young man in Denver who had a business. Before I was through, I ended up with a total of five larger units, and three smaller ones. I eventually sold all of them through auction.

I brought my first newly built unit back to Denver and was excited about the possibilities I knew it would bring. I had carefully planned out that when I did live broadcasts, having a smoker on site to provide delectable, barbequed chicken, ribs, and brisket would be an integral part of the entire package.

I would sell the broadcast portion, then include the signature Daddio cooking where people could see me doing the preparation, and we'd give the food away free. It was a complete and effective promotion piece for KDKO. And true to the beginning of this dream, my first promotion through KDKO using the new cooker was at the grand opening of the light rail in Five Points. We served the free barbeque just as planned and it was a huge success.

That was only the beginning. I continued to do live remotes at area businesses, along with the added promotion of the barbeque that was already built into the price for my advertisers. It was another ongoing journey that continued to evolve and grow.

As with any successful dream, this journey required a lot of hard work. For the promotional broadcasts, I would arrive at the site in the early morning hours, sometimes leaving home at 1 a.m. to set up. It took a lot of time just in the transportation of the equipment; the units were large with the 10 and 20-foot trailers along with a refrigeration truck which was on another tractor trailer.

The unique aspects of these remotes were unreplicable, and well worth the energy. The barbeque was a powerful and memorable tool.

♪♪♪

Over time, some familiar questions from the community began to become louder and more frequent. "How can I find you? Do you have your own restaurant?"

Just as when I had first laid eyes on the smokers in Louisiana, I was once again reminded of Gladys Knight's recommendation from a decade earlier. I began to give more than a notion to the genuine advice from the legendary soul icon I had at one time brushed aside. She had seen something that I wasn't allowing myself to, and it was now time for the world to see it as well.

After all, that's what friends are for.

The smokers at the live remotes were the first step, and I began to sincerely believe I could take all of this to the next level. I had become established in my cooking reputation through the numerous inclusive promotional packages I now had under my belt. The community was asking for our service on a regular basis.

I could hear my mother's voice offering her encouraging refrain, "Buster, you can do anything you set your mind to."

Once again, I believed that I definitely could.

♪♪♪

I took the leap and opened my first restaurant on Oneida Street and East 23rd Avenue in Denver. This first restaurant was very exciting. We were new in the neighborhood and when we cooked, you could smell the delectable aromas for blocks. The scent could be detected all the way to Martin Luther King Boulevard. Everyone knew when we were preparing our feasts.

About four years after the Oneida restaurant opened, I started another restaurant at Buckley and Colfax. This location was regularly patronized by many of the Denver Bronco football players. They would drive through to pick up the food they had ordered in their limousines. We established an excellent working relationship with the NFL franchise, and it was always an honor to serve each one of them.

A few years later, I opened a third restaurant in the nearby town of Bennett that continued for about seven years. I kept the original name in my franchising: Daddio's Kitchen on Wheels. We expanded into the catering business as well.

There used to be many barbeque cook-offs in Denver. One summer day, I was cooking at one of these events. There was a record number of people in attendance, and we ran out of food.

The line of people waiting was all the way around the corner and we had to have additional meat brought from each of the restaurants. At the time, I was operating all three of my locations, on Oneida, on Colfax, and in Bennett.

"Y'all have to wait," I announced to the line of people.

I told the last person in line to not let anyone in line behind them. That didn't work, and the line grew. I counted over two hundred people, and every one of them stayed in line until we were able to restock and catch up.

It was rewarding to realize that our reputation was preceding us.

I would participate in these fairs, but I would never compete in the barbeque contests. I didn't feel like I needed to compete. My product was there, and people could choose to come and get it. My philosophy was that they knew about it and the quality would speak for itself. It was called "Daddio's World-Famous Barbeque" for a reason.

I learned one of the most valuable lessons from my years in the barbeque business. I tell entrepreneurs today that a good product will sell itself. Too often, people focus only on making money in the beginning, without paying attention to the details of what is going to bring them that profit. Then they wonder why they go out of business.

It can't be about "quick money." If you have a quality product, people will make sure they get there to get what they really want.

The reward of community involvement and support is in turn well-earned, and the payoff unfolds exponentially.

At one of the annual Colorado Black Arts Festivals, I was working all afternoon with the smoker feeding the lines of hungry people as I did every year that I had Daddio's Kitchen on Wheels. On this particular day, unbeknownst to me, Dave Segel was sitting under a tree with his family watching me for a long time. Later, he got in line for some food. It had been close to five years since I had last seen him.

He once again complimented me on all that I had achieved. And it once again gave me pause to be recognized for my hard work, and I was grateful to have known him.

12 | Sturgis

"We must reject not only the stereotypes that others hold of us,
but also the stereotypes that we hold of ourselves."

- **Shirley Chisholm**

We did our Soul Cookouts for so many businesses, and this exposure led us to an opportunity to take our product and talents to Sturgis, South Dakota for the Harley-Davidson annual mega event that has become known simply as "Sturgis."

On August 14, 1938, a group of nine men raced their motorcycles with a small group of people watching. These bikers were known as the Jackpine Gypsies Motorcycle Club which later organized the Sturgis Motorcycle Rally. It's turned into the biggest motorcycle rally in the world.

My first time going to Sturgis in 1999 was an experience like no other. It wasn't just the time spent at the South Dakota event; there was a lot of preparation required before even getting there.

Sam's Club was just opening over by Lowry in Denver, and I'm pretty sure I was their first major customer. I purchased all of our meat so we could drive it cross country to an icehouse in Sturgis. An area waited for our arrival, set up to prepare and season the multitude of chicken, ribs and brisket. Everything had to be to code for the health department, and there were licensure agreements to be mindful of.

I didn't rush anything, as I wanted to be sure I crossed all my T's and dotted my I's. It was imperative I was prepared for this adventure I was embarking on.

We drove two motorhomes to accommodate our team the 387 miles to Sturgis. We had a new motorhome for my wife and the young women to stay in and had the other motorhome for the young men and me.

We had three smokers on the flat-bed trailers, and all of our meat awaiting preparation in a refrigeration truck. In addition, we had lemonade machines, corn machines, tables and chairs to transport. We made quite the motorcade traveling across the three states.

Over the course of 17 days, twenty-four/seven, our team cooked for the swarms of people with our three smoker units: the major big cooker at the main location and two smaller units at other surrounding spots.

Our hard-working crew consisted of a total of about 18 people working in shifts. We never had a down moment during that time. There are usually about a million and a half people with motorcycles running all day and night. There is entertainment and music galore, a lot of country and rock.

The small community of Sturgis, with a population of about 6,000 people, is completely transformed for that two and a half weeks. It's amazing that Sturgis can accommodate the mass of people. The entire state of South Dakota nearly doubles its population when the rally bikers, vendors and observers show up each year.

It's an incredibly wild atmosphere. People are running around half naked, sometimes fully nude, and the campgrounds are known for their parties.

When everyone is gone, the landscape is back to cow pastures, a post office, a co-op store, and mom-and-pop operations. The local residents make enough on their rentals to make it through the rest of the year.

After it was all over and we arrived back in Denver, I took about five days just to rest: literally sleeping for two solid days!

We repeated that trip for five years in a row. The only business event where I really lost money was the last year at Sturgis in 2003. It was the 100th anniversary celebration of Harley-Davidson, and it was a different set-up from the previous years when there were rallies at various locations and times throughout the span of the event.

Instead, there was a ten-day gap between the main rally and the celebration of the anniversary. Everyone was traveling to Milwaukee, Wisconsin, the home of the Harley-Davidson company which left a more vacant Sturgis.

We stuck it out, but it was an unanticipated disappointment.

Participating in Sturgis was always grueling, but also a lot of fun. A consequence of all the hard work of those trips, along with the year-round work I did to ensure the success of Daddio's Kitchen on Wheels, is my ongoing back problem and my difficulty walking.

What made it all worthwhile for me was the opportunity to demonstrate firsthand to young people, that if you want something in life, you can make it happen and you have to work for it. Nobody is just going to give it to you.

13 | Ongoing RV Journey

"Don't count the days, make the days count."

- Muhammad Ali

Patsy and I began our recreational vehicle (RV) adventures about 50 years ago, a collection of unforgettable journeys evolving from a small camper to a true RV.

Being a country boy and growing up on the farm, I always enjoyed spending time outdoors. My mom taught me this appreciation of the beauty and peace of nature - the simplicity of this world. In my adult life, fishing and hunting became my hobbies and they brought me a great deal of contentment.

After we moved to Colorado, we'd go out to Cherry Creek Reservoir in Aurora with our young children every weekend for a picnic with our little camper, a shell on the back of the pick-up truck. That picnicking and fishing was our introduction to camping.

As the years went by, we moved higher up the recreational vehicle rungs to a Class C motorhome, built with a cab or cut-away chassis, providing a front structure that looks like a van.

Every week at the radio station, I was advertising for Burt Chevrolet -they were one of my heavy sponsors. Burt Chevrolet started selling motorhomes, so I bought one. That is when the RV hobby really took off, evolving into a lifestyle that we could hardly get enough of.

We'd go every chance we had and would take the kids to the lake, to the park, or camping. After Yolanda, Ricky, Michael, and Jasmine grew up, Patsy and I began to travel more widely in our upgraded comfortable "home away from home."

♪♪♪

A highlight of driving around the country in an RV is the number of interesting people you meet. Some of these people become life-long friends and have an impact on our lives beyond measure.

One of these individuals is Bryan VanLoenen. Pat and I were driving through Kansas when we experienced some always dreaded RV trouble; a piece of the boat hitch had broken off. A woman at a catfish spot where we stopped for lunch told us about a great mechanic who lived down the road and she contacted him to see if he would be able to help.

Before long, a man pulled up in his truck, eager to assist me with our hitch issue. He was able to fix it in short order. I invited him into the RV, and we struck up an easy conversation. Bryan and I soon discovered we had a mutual appreciation of fishing, and from there we connected on many levels.

Whenever Pat and I would be traveling in the region, we would visit Bryan and his parents. Our friendship continued to grow by leaps and bounds. Over the years, I learned he would do anything in the world for me. When I had my farm in Bennett, Colorado, Bryan drove all the way from Kansas to build a fence for me, fenceposts and all. The first year we embarked on our annual Sturgis vending venture, he surprised us and drove all night from Bogue, Kansas, appearing at the house early in the morning, ready and willing to come along and help. He was by my side, sometimes physically and always emotionally, during the difficult time of Pat's illness. This close friend, whom I never would have met if it weren't for that fateful day we had a broken RV hitch, sat with the family at Pat's memorial service in Denver.

Bryan is so genuine and kind, and a rare gem in my life.

♪♪♪

On our frequent RV trips, driving from place to place, I noticed I never seemed to see any Black people with RVs, on the road or anywhere in the various states we went to.

When we were living in Arizona, I had a couple friends who had motorhomes and I was telling them that I hadn't seen any Blacks over the years with this same RV hobby. One of them asked if I'd heard of the National African American RVer's Association (NAARVA).

"That's the organization you need to join. Then your observation would definitely change."

My friend gave me the website, and a few months later he asked if I had checked it out. I told him I had briefly looked it up but hadn't pursued making any kind of contact yet. He and his wife took it upon themselves to get me and Pat registered.

"There's no time like the present," he told me with a smile.

After we moved back to Denver, Pat and I decided we should attend one of the NAARVA rallies. There happened to be a national rally in Missouri that coincided with my vacation time. As we drew closer to the rally location, nothing seemed to have changed in the department of seeing any color inside a motorhome on our journey.

I even asked some people along the way, and the reply was the same, "No, we haven't seen any people of color either."

I was reminded of our first few days after moving to Denver all those years ago, and I said to Pat, "I don't know, maybe we're totally off track, or maybe NAARVA isn't really our answer after all."

Just then, as we turned another corner, I saw a brown arm sticking out of the window of the RV behind us. I was finally convinced we were on the right road, and my hope came flooding back to me.

Suddenly, I caught sight of a sea of motorhomes in front of us. We pulled into the area, and three Brothers had me follow them to get to our RV site. These gentlemen were so helpful, getting everything set up for us. It was like a whole new world had opened up to me and I was like a little boy with a new toy.

NAARVA grew from a group of acquaintances in 52 rigs in 1993 at a place called Winton Woods Campground outside Cincinnati, Ohio, to a membership today in excess of 1500 active RVers. There are now more than 50 local charters of affiliated chapters around the nation.

Annual rallies are held every spring for each of the four geographic regions of NAARVA: Central, Eastern, Southern, and Western. Our region covered eight states. A national camp rally for NAARVA is held every year. Rallies provide fun-filled activities, cultural experiences, and hands-on seminars on a variety of topics related to RVing.

This amazing organization also gives back through its annual scholarship program. College-bound graduating high school seniors who are children or grandchildren of NAARVA members are eligible to apply for financial assistance of $500 and $1,000 scholarships.

We continued enjoying our newfound involvement with NAARVA.

When it came time to elect new organizational officers, Pat ran for secretary. I initially didn't have a desire to be involved at that level, but I found out they were looking for a National Promotions Director.

Well, that's who I am and what I do, so I accepted the position.

NAARVA remained an important part of our lives. We were blessed with the opportunity to visit so many different states with the two rallies, regional and national, that we participated in every year. Pat was secretary for about 17 years. I was off and on with my own involvement during that time since I had so many other irons in the fire.

Joellen Davis is currently the president of our Colorado chapter. Our chapter is called the Rocky Mountain RV Rollers. Over the last several decades we all came together in organizing the club. Joellen and Patsy were on the board of the national NAARVA organization together. Ms. Davis has always been an amazing leader for us.

Over the years, we had fought so hard to have a national rally nearby us. The rallies were always happening across the country - nothing under 1000 miles away from Denver. In 2021, NAARVA finally held a national rally in Gillette, Wyoming - only 343 miles away. I hadn't been at a rally since the last one Pat and I attended three years before. Since it was a fraction of the distance away as previous rallies, I wanted to see friends in the organization that I hadn't seen for a long time and be around that energy again. My two grandsons agreed to go with me, so we embarked on our road trip adventure.

There were 500 people at the 2021 national rally with about 250 units. I hadn't seen these people in several years and it was like a family reunion. It had been 21 years since Pat and I first joined this amazing organization that created new bonds with African Americans from all over the country sharing similar interests and hobbies, and yet each having their own individual way of life, people we would never have met otherwise.

I enjoyed the experience, and at the same time, I felt sad being in the audience for the event programs and not seeing Pat on that stage. That void impacted me more than I anticipated, and I was unable to take part in all the activities because I needed the time on my own, to remember and reflect.

RVing can be very expensive and it's important to have a commitment to the outdoors and a desire to be around all different kinds of people. There were lots of opportunities and ups and downs with the various trips: RV breakdowns, other stressful moments along the way, and then so much fellowship and laughter.

I would love to be RVing full-time if my health would allow it. I would sell my house and hit the road to meet new people and encounter new adventures. But for now, at least, the indelible impressions and recollections will have to suffice.

Thank you, National African American RVers Association, for the incredible memories.

14 | Radio Post KDKO: KUVO and AM 760 Progressive Talk Radio

"If they don't give you a seat at the table, bring a folding chair."

- Shirley Chisholm

When my granddaughter, Lindsay, was about five years old, her mother, Yolanda, would pick her up from Watch-Care Academy and bring her over to KDKO. I would be on the air doing the drive-time announcements and playing the line-up of songs. Lindsay would sit on my lap in the control room, watching me do my thing at the station.

One day when I had to leave the control room for a phone call, I was rushing back before the end of the song.

I was greeted by a small voice reassuring me, "Now, Papa, I can handle it."

Lindsay was sitting there wearing the headset and working the board, calm and cool as a cucumber. It was as if she was born to be on the air, with an experienced demeanor from absorbing all her observations.

The song ended, and this kindergartner's clear, sweet voice was heard over the airwaves. Everybody who was listening was just blown away.

Lindsay began doing on-air public service announcements. By the time she was nine years old, "Miss Thang" had become a regular on KDKO with her own show at 4 p.m. on Mondays, Wednesdays and Fridays.

The artist Monica had recently released her title track, "Miss Thang." Lindsay liked the song so much she adopted the designation as her radio name. The title soon became synonymous to the youngest DJ in Denver.

In 2005, almost three years after selling KDKO, I took on hosting a Saturday blues and jazz show from 7 p.m. to 9 p.m. on KUVO, the Denver jazz public radio station in Five Points. To make time and room for the show in a blues heavy Saturday, KUVO shifted the *R&B Jukebox* that had been in that time slot to an occasional special instead of a weekly staple.

Our jazz and blues show was really Miss Thang's show. By this time, that little girl had turned 18 years old. We were quite a team, the Blues Man and Miss Thang. I wanted to keep my young, self-assured granddaughter exposed on the radio so she would continue to be known, and so she could keep doing what she enjoyed. I remained at KUVO for about four years.

KUVO has an interesting history as well. In 1982, a few dedicated volunteers began working toward their vision of founding a Hispanic-managed public radio station. The well-known Five Points fixture became a reality, offering a mix of fusion jazz, salsa and blues. The station continues in that rich foundation

The program director when I joined the station staff, Carlos Lando, started as a KDKO disc jockey. After moving to Denver in 1980, Carlos spent five years as music and program director and mid-day host at KDKO. After working a year for KBCO in Boulder, he began his journey with KUVO in 1987. Carlos became the president and general manager of KUVO in 2012 and remains committed to providing culturally diverse programs with significant appeal to Latino and African American communities.

♪♪♪

About two years after leaving KUVO, I decided I really wanted to once again be a part of talk radio. I had a lot of things I wanted to say, and I missed being on the airwaves; a platform giving me the opportunity to be the voice of the community.

I applied to KKZN AM 760, Progressive Talk, located in the Tech Center in South Denver, and they hired me to do a two-hour talk radio show. Every Saturday afternoon at 3 p.m. for nearly five years, I hosted *Talking with Dr. Daddio.*

It was exciting to be back in a studio interviewing and meeting people, rather than just announcing and playing jazz at KUVO. I had an opportunity to have conversations with such a wide spectrum of the community, all ethnicities and walks of life.

I interviewed authors, politicians, community activists, fire fighters, police chiefs, teachers, and countless others. It was a great creative outlet. I was in charge of all the planning, and 90% of the preparation, for my show.

For those five years, I was honored to learn and share what was happening in our community, dealing with local issues, and going the extra mile to put the radio station out front to fight the battles for people who needed their voices to be heard.

It was a good opportunity and a great experience for me to be able to do all-talk programming for those two hours each week. The love and support of the community throughout the years was fantastic. *Talking with Dr. Daddio* was designed to enlighten our community – to celebrate it, to help find solutions to its challenges, and to highlight its history. I was able to talk with leaders, introduce new people, and sadly, sometimes give goodbye tributes.

There were many organizations I was able to help give needed exposure and connect with other resources. One of the many organizations I will never forget is Shades of Blue; comprised of pilots, educators and business leaders dedicated to mentoring and arranging internship and employment referrals for young people who desire to pursue science, technology, engineering and math (STEM) careers, primarily focused on aviation and aerospace.

Captain Willie Daniels, the founder, CEO and president of Shades of Blue, was a United Airlines pilot for more than 30 years. Captain Daniels introduced the Shades of Blue STEM program over 20 years ago on KDKO. Captain Daniels is one of the greatest leaders I have met.

I was honored to have the many guests that we brought to the radio station on my program. I had the amazing opportunity through AM 760 to interview 14 of our country's Black astronauts nearly a decade ago including Dr. Guion Bluford, the first Black astronaut to launch into space; Dr. Mae Jemison, the first Black woman to travel in space; and Dr. Bernard A. Harris, Jr, the first Black man to walk on the moon.

On August 15, 2015, Shades of Blue held their Gala dinner and astronaut reunion at Wings over the Rockies Air & Space Museum in Denver. This reunion was one of the most exciting experiences of my life. I felt honored, and I will never forget having the opportunity to see these astronauts, talk with them and shake their hands. Fourteen Black astronauts attended this reunion. It was the first time they had ever been all together in the same room.

Renowned Denver sculptor Ed Dwight was celebrated as well. Ed Dwight opened the door for all Black astronauts when he was chosen in the early 1960s by President John F. Kennedy to enter training to become the first Black astronaut candidate - becoming a fully qualified Aerospace Research Pilot, before switching career paths.

I felt that every media outlet in the world should have been at this event. Theirs are the stories that you rarely hear about. NASA has commissioned over 300 astronauts into space since 1958, and the number of Black astronauts is now at 24 in 2022, three have passed on.

I was also grateful to the radio station to give me the opportunity to meet President Obama in person and shake his hand on one of his Denver visits.

Over time, I saw changes coming with the format of the station. Progressive radio was being eliminated across the country with the swing back to the conservative movement. Progressive is not where we are at our foundation.

Sadly, AM 760 changed its format to all sports talk. Sports is not my expertise and in turn, not a way to serve my community that continues to need a voice.

15 | Fair Share Jobs

"If you have no confidence in self, you are twice defeated in the race of life."

- Marcus Garvey

Practically all my life I have been concerned with helping people find jobs, assisting people in my community any way I can.

When I was doing my weekly progressive talk radio show at AM 760, I was invited to be the moderator on a panel in Montbello for a meeting of a local chapter of the National Association for the Advancement of Colored People. We had representatives on the panel from all walks of life: the Denver Police Department, the mayor's office, clergy, activists, the area NAACP president and other members, among others.

I was very happy to see the response from the community that evening. As I was moderating and looking out at the audience, I was pleased to see some very identifiable figures, people and leaders I hadn't seen in years. I realized that there were many mature and seasoned people who were interested in creating a change, and who wanted to work with the community again.

Larry Borom was one of those individuals who was at this panel discussion, and I was reminded of his positions with various Urban Leagues over the years: in Minnesota, Michigan, New York City, and then Denver. Larry had also served as a human rights director with the city of Denver, as well as chairman of the Black Education Advisory Council. He was a strong advocate for role models that looked like and represented our youth.

Following the discussion, Larry and I migrated towards one another to catch up. It was good to connect with the life-long teacher and activist and our conversation naturally evolved towards the possibility of collaborating to serve our community again in some form. I was impressed with the responses and reactions from several others as well that fateful night.

One of the main ideas we discussed was the need for jobs in the Black community. With the combined wisdom and experience of Larry's leadership with the Urban League and my past leadership with KDKO, we created an organization to serve this purpose called Fair Share Jobs.

Others who were involved in the ongoing conversation, including our organization accountant Geneva Smith-Doss and Andre Wilkins, joined Larry and I for this common goal. Our plain and "simple" theme was to get Black folk in our community the jobs they needed and deserved.

We met for about five months to create our plan and to find a location for our endeavor. One of our requirements was to find someone who could provide a gratis facility. Carl Bourgeois came to my mind – an entrepreneur and owner of several properties in the Five Points neighborhood.

When I approached Mr. Bourgeois with my hopeful request, he shared with me that he had at least one empty building.

"Daddio, I'll do what I can to help," he said. "We're thinking about doing some remodeling and right now, this particular building isn't being used," he continued. "Until I get ready to do some work on it, you can have an office there."

We set up shop in Five Points. We stayed in that space for a year while we worked through the various kinks and all that is involved in structuring a new operation. Larry invited Billy Scott, who is now a Denver real estate agent, to join our organization and he was also a good fit, bringing in his own expertise.

The next step was to obtain our 501c3 status. I went to Wayne Vaden, an attorney who I respect a great deal. We got our money together for the application process for a Colorado non-profit organization. Wayne completed the application for us, we were accepted, and Fair Share Jobs was off and running.

It was time to narrow down our specified projects for our planned scope of work. Through our research, we discovered there were no Black workers on the metro area light rail or local Amtrak at the time. We wanted to get involved to help remedy the situation.

We actively pursued an appointment to meet with Mayor Michael Hancock to see how we could become a part of the existing light rail project. We were finally able to secure an appointment with Mayor Hancock's deputy chief of staff, Stephanie O'Malley, and another executive from his office.

We never heard back from them after that meeting, except to receive a letter explaining that there was nothing they could do to help us with getting a contract.

"We aren't trying to get no jobs or contracts," I exclaimed. "We're trying to put people on these jobs!"

I was feeling exasperated. "I don't live in Denver anymore so I'm going to talk to the Aurora officials where I do live."

I went and talked with Aurora Mayor Steve Hogan who had become a good friend of mine. I was armed and ready with information and a plan - brochures and the works. The meeting went well, and the door was opened.

"Let me get with City Council and get back to you," Steve said.

Within the week, Mayor Hogan was back in touch with me.

"How would you like to do this?" he asked.

"Well, first we need an office," were the first words out of my mouth.

He pondered my request for a moment and said, "Maybe we can put your organization within the City and County system. There's quite a bit of open office space right now."

Mayor Hogan talked with the necessary people and Fair Share Jobs was on the agenda for practically every upcoming City Council meeting. We would receive calls about various facilities that were available for us to look at.

One offer was for a space near the Community College of Aurora, but it just wasn't the right site. Then someone else offered a place off Chambers Road that was too small. None of these locations were quite the right fit.

Until a call came in for a place off Iliff Avenue in Aurora. We discovered it was a facility being used at the time by the Aurora Parks and Recreation Department. They were in the process of relocating. It was an actual house and it seemed like an ideal place, inside and out. There was a beautiful park next door where we could hold job fairs. It was overall a great spot.

The Parks and Rec people moved out and Fair Share Jobs moved in. We were there until the next election cycle. Even though most of the Aurora City Council continued to be supportive, we ended up being asked to move out, because there were new council members who claimed they were not aware there were buildings that were being used by non-profit organizations. We sensed that wasn't true, and that it was a way to get us out. It felt like we were back at square one.

We ended up making a move to a shopping center off Alameda and Sable in Aurora, thanks to arrangements made once again by Mayor Hogan and members of his staff. We remained there until, in 2018, developers decided to remodel every space in the complex and build apartment buildings. Every business had to move out. The area is no longer even recognizable as it once had been.

When that happened, I decided to let it all go. Fair Share Jobs had thrived for seven years. It was taking a great deal of my energy as I had become the sole coordinator, with a few trusty and supportive volunteers to help with daily operations.

There were so many building projects in the Denver Metro area and African Americans seemed rarely to be involved or employed. Fair Share Jobs tried to change that reality. We were able to put people to work from many different walks of life in a variety of types of jobs, particularly in the booming field of construction.

We had a very strong and successful system in our organization. In that seven years, Fair Share Jobs ended up giving between 3,000 and 4,000 individuals some form of active employment. This will always be a great source of pride for me. We had support from the police department, the fire department, the City and County of Aurora, Parks and Recreation, and many other community organizations.

I will always appreciate Mayor Hogan's strong involvement. He was always very concerned and in support of what we were trying to accomplish. Steve continued to work on every angle in helping us out, for as long as he was in office. Without his belief in what we were doing, we wouldn't have had our long success in Aurora.

A large part of Fair Share Jobs involved training: the process of building a resume, how to dress, how to interview successfully, the strategies in approaching an employer. We practiced role plays so job seeking individuals felt prepared and ready to handle many different types of situations.

One of many success stories was a young man who was referred by one of the volunteers in the office. His mother was a good friend of ours.

He came in looking sharp, wearing his suit and tie. It was one of those situations that could be called an oxymoron. This young man had on a suit that would be fitting for a stock market interview. I was so impressed. It turns out he was looking for a diesel mechanic job.

I got on the phone with someone at RTD and told her about this unique young man. When he went in for his mechanic interview, he was dressed in the same manner.

He became a successful RTD mechanic, doing exactly what he wanted to do. He was so intelligent and goal oriented. That was one of my most remarkable and memorable experiences in my rewarding chapter with Fair Share Jobs.

There were of course those we couldn't help. There was such a marked contrast when someone came in to apply for a job and didn't really want it. I could tell almost immediately if their visit was motivated by pressure from a partner or family member. It demonstrated how key it is to truly want help. It doesn't happen automatically, and people must be willing to work for what they want.

It wasn't only with employment that we were helping people. We had a wide referral list for many different services and needs, and people turned to us for all kinds of advice.

A woman came in asking for a good attorney recommendation.

"I'm trying to find an attorney who can help me," she explained. "I spent almost $5,000, and these people are just trying to railroad me."

The first number I gave her unfortunately turned her away, telling her they could not help her.

Not to be deterred myself, I called someone to get a more specialized referral. She called this person and had an appointment the next day.

Two weeks later, the woman came back into our office and hugged me.

"I just want to thank you," she exclaimed. "That attorney wrote one letter to clear things up and didn't charge me a penny!"

It just goes to show that sometimes it takes some perseverance on all sides. If we didn't have the answer for someone, we would find a way to get it. A major key to success was connecting people with appropriate resources and helping them with preparedness.

Our goal was to reach the top, and we had the desire to help the community in any way we were able. Our hearts were truly in what we were trying to accomplish.

Fair Share Jobs made a big impression on our community, on the city of Aurora, and on the state of Colorado. It is my hope that someone who is young and committed may someday come forward and step up for me to pass the torch and return Fair Share Jobs to a functioning operation once again, carrying on an important and vital legacy.

I'd like to believe the organization is just on a pause, and that it can be continued and taken to a new level one day. That would make me so proud. I continue to keep up to date with the necessary filings to maintain the 501c3 non-profit status.

16 | Asphalt Sealant Business

"Never be limited by other people's limited imaginations."

- Dr. Mae Jemison

Another business I feel was a valuable asset and made a difference in many lives was my venture in asphalt and roof repair, J Walker Construction Company.

As always, I kept my eyes open for opportunities and ways to better the lives of others in the community even though my plate was full with my ownership of KDKO, concert promotions, and Daddio's Kitchen on Wheels.

I had heard about a company called Southwestern Petroleum Corporation based in Fort Worth, Texas. It sounded legitimate and pretty amazing, so I looked into it a little more and on one of my trips to Louisiana, I set up a meeting with a guy from the company in Dallas.

I started asking him questions about what set this business apart.

"We specialize in water proofing systems and protective coatings."

My new friend went on to explain. "We manufacture steel coated sealant, and any roof we do, we guarantee it for 15 years."

As we continued our conversation, I became more and more fascinated and intrigued by the uniqueness of this seeming world-renowned organization. I asked him to send me some more literature and I continued with my own research.

I couldn't get Southwestern Petroleum out of my mind.

Marketed under SWEPCO, their brand has been helping provide reliable, long-term, cost-effective waterproofing solutions for industrial and commercial roofs since 1933. The corporation got its start during the great depression and began with only six employees.

Their array of incredible products included protective coatings, primers, sealers, reinforcing membranes and patching materials manufactured with unique ingredients referred to as a "cold process." In addition to roofs, their product line helped maintain floors, walls, metal and pavement. They claimed these were products of unmatched performance.

Not only the apparent quality, but their company philosophy made a lot of sense to me. Because much of the cost of commercial and industrial maintenance goes to the labor required to install the products, it seemed logical to specify the best products available so maintenance could be performed less frequently. Southwestern Petroleum prided themselves in long service life, reduced application costs, energy savings, reduced maintenance costs, environmentally friendly formulations and freedom from problems.

The visions for possibilities and potential began spinning and snowballing in my mind. I was certain this would be a good avenue for young people to be put to work and gain employment. I knew a lot of young men who wanted to work, but they were unable to get hired anywhere.

Back in Colorado, I continued in deeper conversation with the guy who was my source and connection to this company. Like so many of my life endeavors, this one felt orchestrated through destiny and a higher power.

This gentleman sent me some product samples and I began by finding contacts at the Colorado Department of Transportation (CDOT) in both Denver and Castle Rock.

After I gave them my presentation, they said they had heard of SWEPCO, but they informed me "the product was too good for them."

Not long after my meeting with the highway department, I received a call from a maintenance director in Castle Rock.

"I have a problem with a leaky roof from melting snow, and I'd be willing to try your petroleum product."

I drove to Castle Rock to meet with him. I went inside his shop, and he showed me how it was leaking. I had learned what to look for with the seams and went up on the roof. Then, I applied the SWEPCO product and stopped it from leaking.

"When winter is over, I'll come back and we'll do the roof," I told him as I left.

Before the end of the season, he called me once again and told me there were a couple cracks. I took my crew over there to fill the cracks, and you couldn't tell there had ever been any issue.

I received another call from him, and I could tell he had now been influenced by his boss at CDOT.

"We can't buy this product because you will put me out of work," was his opening greeting.

Obviously, the product they were currently using did not have long lasting results. They would have to patch again in another six months, and he needed to keep people working.

Next, I approached Amoco, a line of gas stations that disappeared over 20 years ago. I ended up getting a contract to do all the seal coatings and fix any roof problems for 167 service stations across Pueblo, Colorado Springs, Denver and Cheyenne, Wyoming. I had a crew of about 40 young men with four trucks.

One of the best parts about this business was I didn't have to worry about credit checking or bill collecting. In just seven days, our product was delivered to the service station address having been pre-paid. All our people had to do was roll up in the truck and perform the process of sealing.

Southwestern had contests among their salespeople, and their top selling people could take vacations to conferences and workshops. It was their way of showing appreciation for their team from all over the country. On top of a great business venture, Pat and I were able to enjoy some nice trips.

I continued growing this business for about five years until I made my move to Arizona. It was an exciting experience, and a great employment opportunity for a number of young people. I was paying from 11 to 12 dollars an hour at that time. My two sons worked for me in the business as well.

It was a great opportunity for anyone who wanted to do something with their hands. There was a lot of manual labor involved, as was the case with so many of my business choices.

It's amazing to me Southwestern Petroleum Corporation isn't more widely known and recognized. Looking back, that truly was one of the greatest businesses I have had.

17 | Artesian Water Business

"The man with no imagination has no wings."

- Muhammad Ali

I grew up on an oil field in Louisiana.

When I was about 12 years old, they drilled into our ground, and rather than hitting oil, they hit water. It was an artesian water well, and that simple error set in motion a whole new opportunity.

As an adult involved in various other businesses, I thought about tapping into this ready-made well, and after selling KDKO, I began creating plans for an artesian water business with the resource that was gifted to my life.

I have always had a special relationship with water. Even though my astrological sign of Taurus is an earth sign, I'm forever drawn to water. This is most represented by my love of fishing and being able to spend an entire day in a boat or on shore with a line in the water. Water is soothing to me. I can reflect on the issues of life by the water, and I come up with some of my greatest ideas in the shower.

The green of the season is from water. The earth is made up of mostly water. Water can cause great destruction through flooding and its tremendous force. Water has both physical and spiritual power beyond measure. There is nothing living that can survive without water. Water is life.

Artesian water is filtered naturally without the use of chemicals or other processes. This of course, gives it more health benefits and a better taste. Artesian wells provide more water than surface wells, a lower risk of contamination due to being so deep underground, and year-round access to clean water. Pressure in the rocks underground force the water to the surface, so there is no pumping required. When an artesian well is drilled, the pressure is relieved, and the water can find a path to open air.

The first artesian well on record was drilled in 1126, by a group of monks in the French province of Artois. At that time, there were no drilling rigs, so the aquifer had to be reached by brute force; the average depth being 150 feet.

When I made the decision to take the plunge into water sales, I was very inspired, and I was prepared to do all the needed research. As with most of my business plans, my mind was going a hundred miles an hour, formulating all the complex details.

I got on the phone to talk to a guy I had grown up with who ran a fracking company in northern Louisiana. I hadn't seen him in years, and I set up an appointment to meet with him.

As soon as I sat down in his office, he immediately asked me about the artesian water well. He remembered as a child that his mom would bring containers over to fill.

"You sure have a good memory," I remarked.

"We're having a problem," he said. "We need water."

I sat back in my chair, listening carefully to this developing collaboration.

"I'm buying water from Shreveport," he continued. "Half of the time they cut me off because I can't get the water. The city needs it, so I'm in a bind."

After more deliberate conversation, he directed me to a man who had an oil well on his property and owned water trucks. This guy was obviously quite wealthy, and it would take a lot of money to make this plan happen. I knew it was going to be an investment with a number of steps in the process.

First, I went to a guy who had a logging company and told him I needed some trees cut. He assessed the situation and said he couldn't help me as it was too small a job for his two-million-dollar lumber company.

Never to be deterred, I went to see a cousin of mine who owned heavy machinery through his smaller lumber cutting business.

"Could you cut down some trees, and also dig a pond?" I asked him.

I hired him to complete that phase of the project.

After that, I had to put a separate transformer in and run a power line to it. I obtained a specific lining for the pond that would provide lifetime protection for the special water and would never rot. A guy from Texas came and measured for the lining, and the next day a team of people came to install it.

I had to have the water tested to ensure it was safe for every use, including drinking. The first time it was discovered to be high in sodium, so we dug it a little deeper and then the sodium measured well below acceptable levels.

I put all this together in 17 days.

I knew the artesian well was still there. I had previously signed a consent that if anything happened to the well, the gas company would not be responsible. But when they came to drill it again, they couldn't get through the existing concrete. They ended up drilling me a whole new well.

The next thing was to put the pump in and let the water run for two days. After a whirlwind two and a half weeks, I got back in touch with my original contact up north. His people had been pulling water out of lakes and creeks.

I asked him if he was ready to buy water from me.

"I'm ready whenever you are!" He replied.

"You can send your trucks over anytime," I said.

"You're kidding me?" He marveled, incredulously.

It wasn't long before seemingly his whole company was there. There were 18 trucks lined up that very first day. It was obvious there was a need for quality water in the area. I had a float inside the pond, and when it was below the level of the base of the float, it would fill back up.

I had wanted to make sure everything was conducive for the required waiting while the trucks filled, and during the additional required administrative work. There was a canopied area where drivers could have lunch or do their paperwork.

I was down there for two months running the operation. I admit that my head grew almost as big as the pond, and I thought I had arrived.

I had wanted to have my main source of clientele be the forestry service. However, I couldn't get into that industry as my water business wasn't on a large enough scale. I relied on towns and medium size businesses for my water services. I would need corporate demand on a larger scale for it to have truly paid off.

It was then, in 2010, that Obama placed a moratorium on drilling, and it put a halt to our exciting venture. After that, drilling seemed to move to Texas. Now I was encountering unanticipated roadblocks, and my health was beginning to decline as well. I realized I would have to let it go by the wayside, at least for the time being.

I had also always wanted to run water from the well on the home property in the country into Gibsland. The town historically had bad water, and they still do. I had a friend whose father was the mayor, and I was trying to get a grant for all the logistics, but I wasn't successful. There was too much red tape.

I still have all the interest in the world in restarting the artesian water business. It is such good quality water and I worked hard to ensure that it met all the guidelines and specifications. I still think about the opportunity that continues to be there.

It would take a large investment to get the business up and running again. However, the water is still accessible, and the pond is still lined. The water level has gone down because it hasn't had any usage.

Water is a primary resource, and such a precious commodity. Someone once told me, "I need more of that holy water."

If I were just a few years younger, I would try to find the right people to be involved. The land and the well are still there. It is another one of my dreams that never fades.

18 | Youth Fishing Trips

ılı|ılı|ılı 🎤 ılı|ılı|ılı

"The future belongs to those who prepare for it today."

- Malcolm X

For 17 years surrounding my ownership of KDKO, I coordinated an annual summer fishing trip for urban boys over a weekend in June. Upwards of 35 kids would participate in this three-night trip; we would leave on a Thursday and return on Sunday.

I see a lot of these young men around the community now who were a part of this experience. The first thing they usually do is make sure their cap is straight.

Before we would leave, I would have a meeting with their mothers and make sure I was clear on all the instructions for any medications and other special needs. I would tell these parents that I was not a babysitter, and their sons would have to work hard.

I was adamant that I would not tolerate any nonsense. If their child did anything outside the rules or got out of line, I would knock him on his behind. Disrespect would not be tolerated. Respect was key.

When we left on a Thursday, we would always stop at the Army Surplus Store to pick up all our camping supplies and head east across the plains of Colorado. I would make prior arrangements so we could stop at the prison along the way to see the men in the yard. We would talk about the consequences of getting involved in the criminal justice system, and the importance of avoiding that experience at all costs.

When we arrived in the small town of Sterling, Colorado, about 130 miles east of Denver, we would stop for a different sort of education and some levity. One of the museums had an ongoing dinosaur fossil display, and every year they would let my kids sign the papier-mache dinosaur and it would stay there until the next year, demonstrating some consistency and permanence. Many of these kids didn't have much of that, so it offered some security. It was a small gesture that meant a lot.

We'd even stop at a farm so the boys could experience sitting on a tractor and gain more knowledge on the agricultural process. We stopped at the fish hatchery so they could learn about how the fish were stocked in the lake and understand the steps in the entire process. In the afternoon, a late lunch at McDonalds in Sterling was arranged for our hungry crew. We had a full trip even before we made our destination.

When we arrived at Sterling Reservoir, the National Guard would meet us there so they could help and teach our group how to put up their tents. Wildlife personnel would go out on the water with us and teach everyone about the boat and its navigation. In the summer, the reservoir was well stocked with crappie, a delicious panfish, so everyone would catch fish, reinforcing both competence and confidence. We would then drive to the local general store and purchase all the fixings for a fish fry. Thanks to the National Guard furnishing an ice truck, the boys could take their fish home and have a fish fry with their families.

There were no restrooms and no showers. The boys were instructed on the importance of a shovel. Each day everyone had to be up at daybreak. The conditions and expectations were very much like a boot camp. There were countless life lessons contained in each trip with the best kind of learning, hands-on. Over the course of our journey, the boys learned about the important role of spiritualty and prayer.

Occasionally, I would have a problem with one or more of the boys and I would always be direct and upfront with their parents or guardians on our return. I would let the parents and their child know that unless something changed in their specific behaviors, there could be some very serious consequences in the future, with law enforcement or society. I would let them know, without any sugarcoating, their current track was not going to work in the direction it was going.

I remember on one trip I was really tough on this kid who thought he was a real serious gangster. A few of the boys and I had gone to pick up the fish fry supplies and when we returned, the tents were all broken down on the ground. Several of the boys came running up to let me know what had happened, and who was the instigator of the fight that had wreacked so much havoc while we were gone.

When I confronted this young man, he got real smart with me. I grabbed him by his collar, and I took him over to the campfire. His eyes got so big. He believed that I might actually throw him into the flames. He had to apologize to everyone and finish off with a prayer. To reinforce the message through natural consequences for tearing down the tents, I made him sleep outside under the stars that night.

When we returned to Denver, a couple of the trip chaperones

didn't think how I had handled the situation was appropriate, so they didn't hesitate to tell this young man's mom what had happened.

"Daddio was really tough on your son," was the introduction to the report they gave.

His mother came after me and let me have it. She was both protective and furious.

I told her that I should have put him in the fire the way he was conducting himself.

"I told you we would tolerate no disrespect and he broke that rule," I firmly explained to her. "I'm trying to help you raise him, so he doesn't end up at the end of that Cradle-to-Prison pipeline."

That message seemed to sink in.

His mother and I ended up becoming good friends and she accepted my continuing assistance and guidance in her son's life. I like to believe that is a significant part of the reason that his whole life turned around over the course of his teen years. He and I have stayed in touch and now he has a family of his own.

I've enjoyed being a surrogate father and mentor to so many young men over the years, with these fishing trips and in many other valuable mentoring experiences. It has been one of the most rewarding aspects of my life, another avenue to feel like I am making a difference and doing God's ongoing will.

These are contributions I have made to create meaning, to somehow help someone give pause in their life so their own existence can also make a difference.

It's like a domino effect when all the pieces are stacked in alignment. And it's beautiful.

My mother, Mattie (Ludie) Frazier-Walker

My sister, Minnie Walker-Dawson

My brother, Charles Walker

Me as a child

My childhood home in Gibsland, Louisiana

The road to my home

Me as a teenager

My wife, Patsy Ruth Stroman-Walker, at her graduation

Me and Patsy

Yolanda

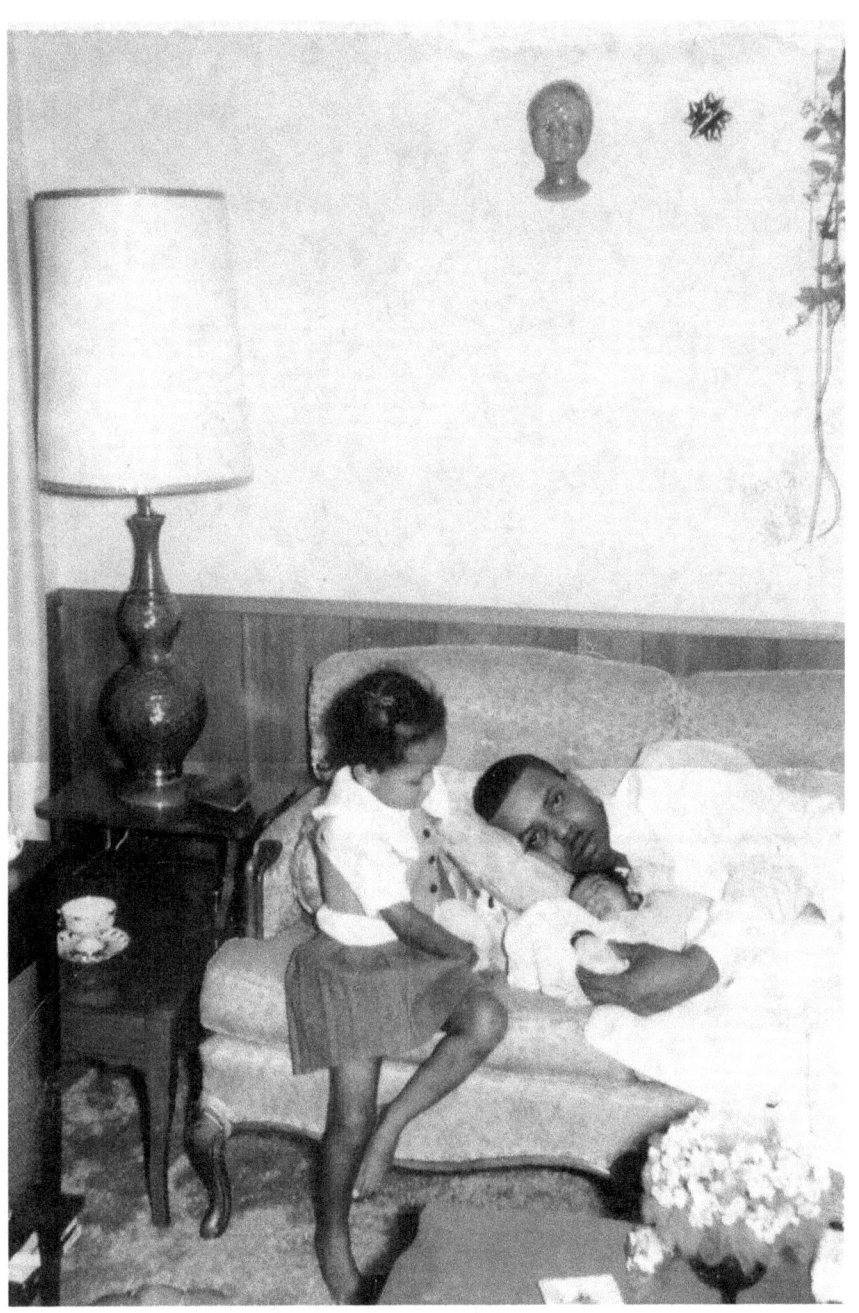

Me with Yolanda and Ricky

Michael, Yolanda, Ricky, me, Pat, and Jasmine

Hero Dad

You are my hero, Dad
You're my secure foundation.
When I think of you, I'm filled with love
And fond appreciation.
You make me feel protected;
I'm sheltered by your care.
You're always my true friend;
When I need you, you're always there.
You have a place of honor
Deep within my heart.
You've been my superhero, Dad,
Right from the very start.

Me and Jasmine

At a KDKO live remote

DR. DADDY-O
4-7

On the air, 4 p.m.- 7 p.m.

Wall of pictures and awards in my office

Radio in my soul

KDKO bumper stickers through the eras

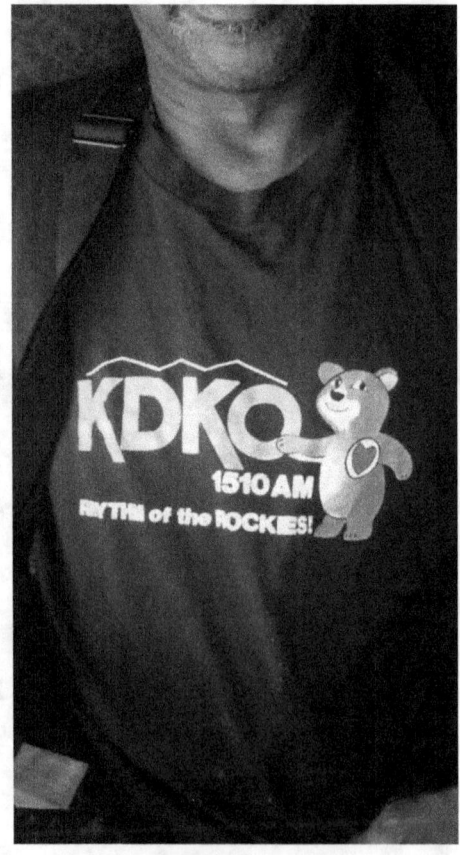

KDKO T-shirt

KDKO DJs

Gladys Knight and the Pips concert

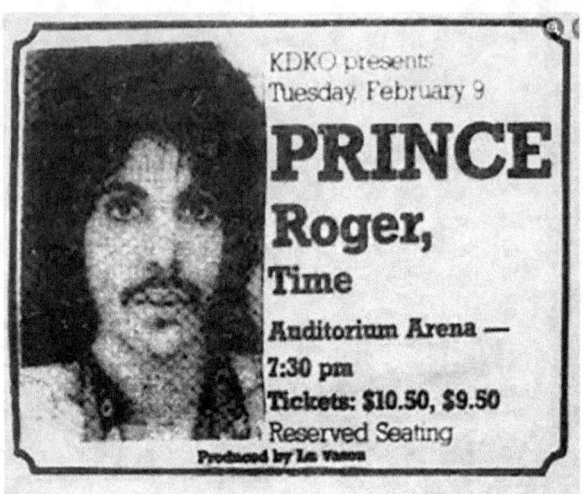

Prince concert

Isley Brothers concert

Johnnie Cochran interview

Sandy Thompson ▶ Denver's 1510 KDKO

KDKO's Sandy Thompson and Muhammad Ali

119

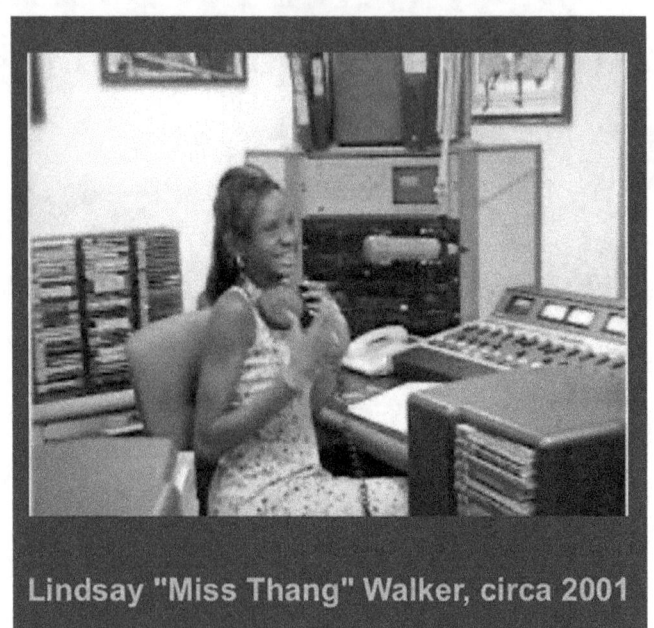

Lindsay "Miss Thang" Walker, circa 2001

James Brown and "Miss Thang"

brother jeff, Lindsay, and the late R&B pop star Aaliyah,
"The Princess of R&B"

Lindsay "Miss Thang" growing up on the air

Lindsay with her Papa

Pat and me

The love of my life

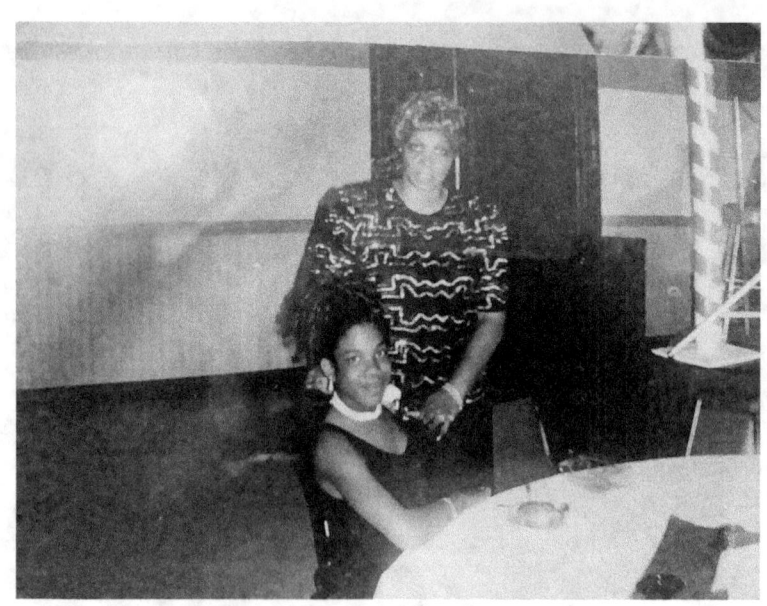

Pat and Jasmine

Pat and me with Alexis at her graduation from DU

J.J., Pat, and Tori

Pat and J.J. dancing at Mr. Norman Harris' 99th birthday party

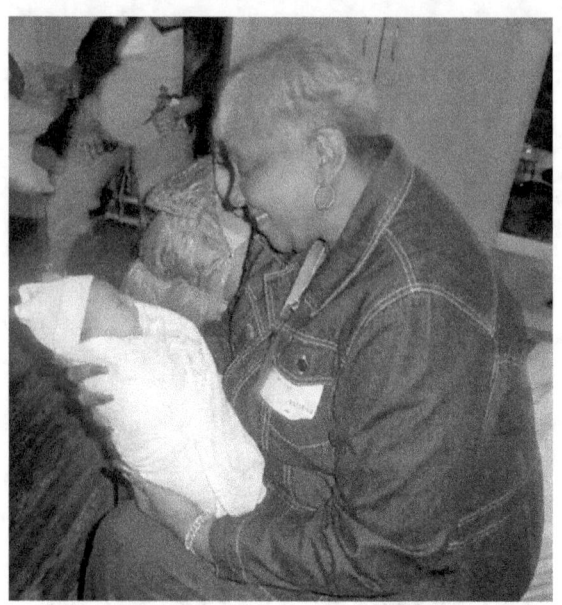

Proud Grandma holding our first great-grandchild,
Xavier (Lindsay's son)

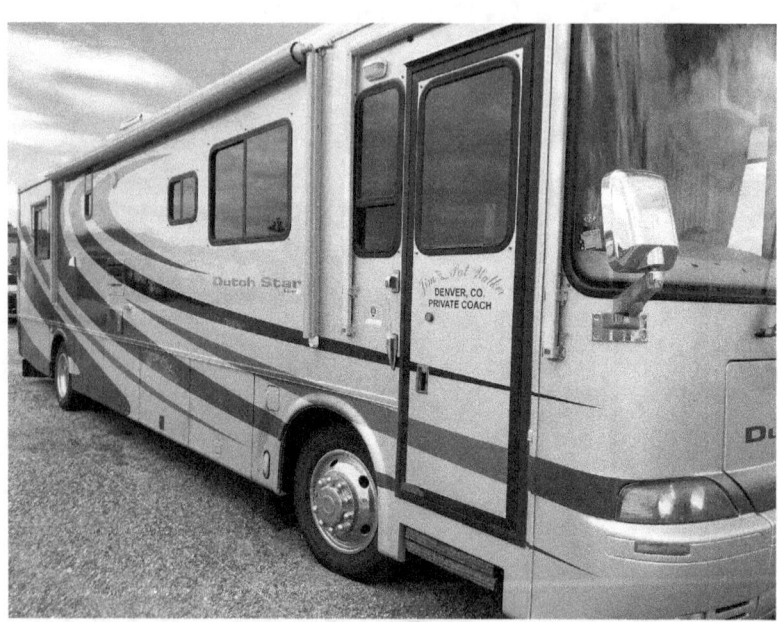

Our RV

Pat

Pat's mom, Leola Stroman

Yolanda, Ricky, Michael, Jasmine, and me with Pat on her birthday

Xavier, me, Pat, Lindsay, and Alexis at
Xavier's basketball game in Dallas

Alexis, me, and Lindsay at Bill Pickett Invitational Rodeo

Tori and me at Cherry Creek Reservoir before
her first Homecoming dance

Giving wisdom to J.J.

Me and J.J. before his first Homecoming dance

Pat with Halle and Tori on a shared birthday celebration

Michael, Jasmine, Pat, me, and Harris at
Harris' birthday celebration

Alexis, Halle, Pat, and Lindsay at Halle's
graduation from South High School

The family celebrating my birthday at Welton Street Cafe

My Deacon Ordination at Ebenezer Baptist Church. Back row: Michael, Harris, Jennifer (Michael's wife), Halle, Alexis, Lindsay, Yolanda, Ricky, Jasmine, Warren Jamison (my second cousin). Front row: Aryana, Pat, me, Tori, Xavier, and J.J.

Pat's last birthday celebration.
Back row: Jennifer, Michael, Jasmine, me, Pat, Yolanda, Tori, Halle,
Alexis, Lindsay, Lawrence McCain (Lindsay's husband).
Front row: Harris, J.J., Ricky, Aryana, Angelle (friend).

Tyler Jackson (Alexis' husband), Alexis, me, and Xavier
the evening of Tyler's proposal

With my great-grandson, Levi (Lindsay's second son)

Yolanda, Ricky, Jasmine, and me

137

Norma Paige, Bee Harris, me, and Pat at The Kasbah
- Photo courtesy of Denver Urban Spectrum

Michael Jackson impersonator, me, and Pat
- Photo courtesy of brother jeff

Yolanda, Alexis, Lindsay, Pat, Minnie, and me

Machelle, me, and Minnie

Me and Machelle

Me, Alexis, Lindsay, Yolanda, Lawrence, and Xavier

Xavier, J.J., Lindsay, Tori, Aryana, Alexis, Tyler, and me

J.J., Aryana, Jasmine, and Tori

Xavier, Lindsay, Kirk Dunham (Lindsay's and Alexis' father),
Alexis, me, Levi, Yolanda, Tyler at Alexis' graduation from the
University of Iowa College of Law

Denver Urban Spectrum Men of Distinction, Fathers of Wisdom honorees and acceptors June 2014. Left to right: Dr. Collis Johnson, Jr., Dr. Russ Simpson, Charles Burrell, Dr. Johnny Johnson, Jr., Ed Dwight, Roland "Fatty" Taylor, Doyle James, Lawrence Pierre, Bruce Gipson, Bee Harris, Maurice Wade, Herman Malone, me, LaDorria Jones, and Moses Brewer - Photo courtesy of Denver Urban Spectrum

Moses Brewer presenting me with my Men of Distinction award - Photo courtesy of Denver Urban Spectrum

Landri Taylor, Roger Kilgore, brother jeff, me, Michael Kiley, and
Dr. Dwinita Mosby Tyler at a school board debate on AM 760
- Photo courtesy of brother jeff

Me at AM 760 studio - Photo courtesy of brother jeff

Unidentified, Joslyn Davis, Geneva Smith-Doss, me, unknown, Pastor Terrence "Big T" Hughes, brother jeff at Fair Share Jobs office - Photo courtesy of brother jeff

Black Men in Support of Education at a Denver elementary school visit - Photo courtesy of brother jeff

At Smiley Middle School in Park Hill Denver
- Photo courtesy of brother jeff

With Denver City Councilwoman Candi CdeBaca at 2022 Five
Points Jazz Festival - Photo courtesy of brother jeff

In the Five Points Jazz Festival parade with Candi.
I was the grand marshal.

With Norman Harris III at the 2022 Juneteenth Music Festival

Juneteenth channel 7 news interview with Rob Harris

Yolanda, me, Alexis, and Lindsay at Hazel Miller performance at 2022 City Park Jazz

Fishing with Pastor Reginald Holmes and brother jeff

My catches

Pat's picture on my special walking stick

At home

Volume 22, Number 12, Feb. 2009

denver urban SPECTRUM

spreading the news about people of color

Black History
Radio Icon
Jim "Dr. Daddio"
Walker
... Page 4

2009 African
Americans
Who Make A
Difference
... Page 17

President Barack
Obama Special:
Presidential
Inauguration
Coverage
... Page 19

Illustration by Drew Mannie

Mannie 4/09

I got top billing over President Obama on the cover

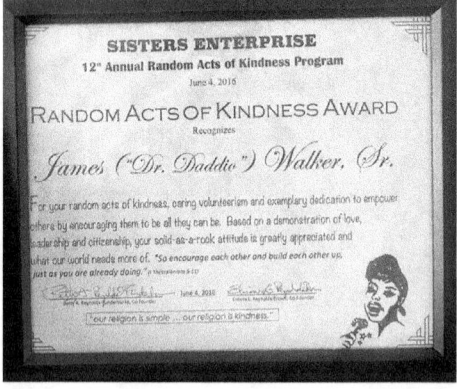

Awards

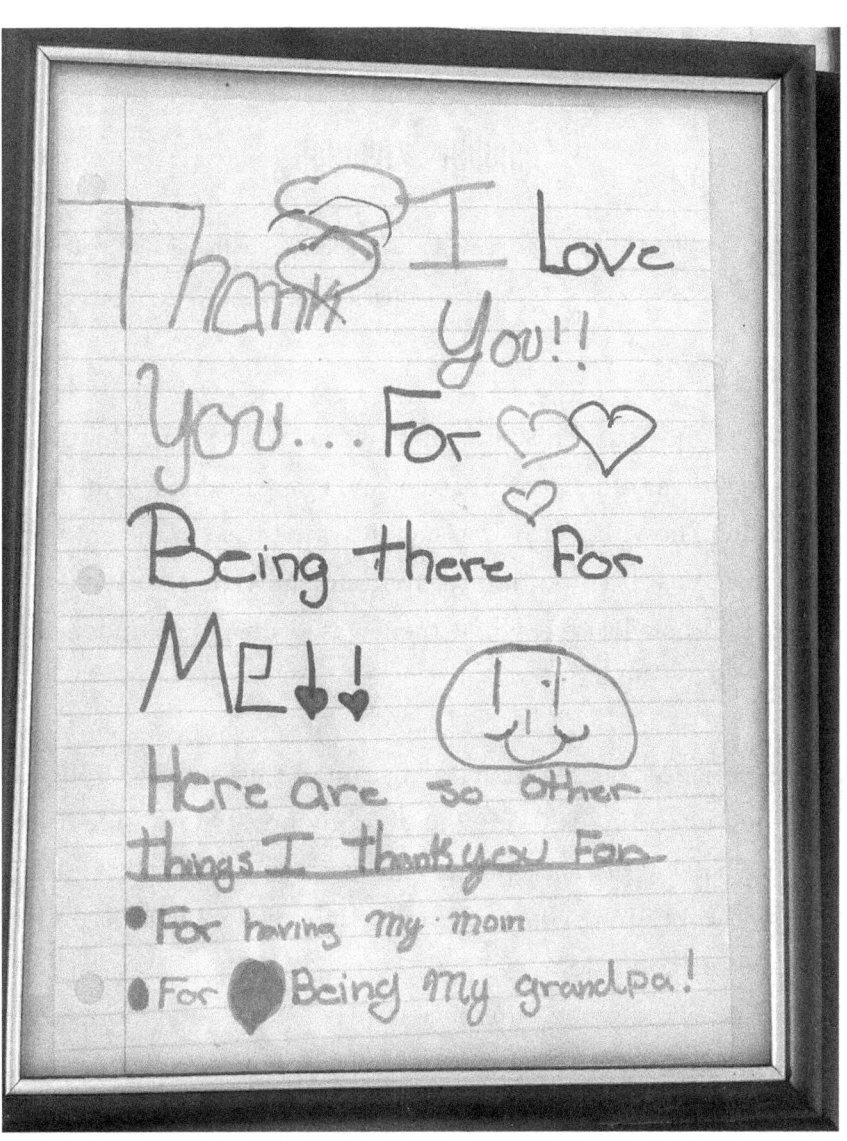

My best award of all - from Tori

19 | Race and Discrimination

"Our lives begin to end the day we become silent about things that matter."

- Dr. Martin Luther King, Jr.

I didn't understand discrimination when I was a young child. I just thought the way other people of color and I were treated was the norm.

I didn't know the term "racism." It wasn't used in the era I was growing up, at least not in my environment. When I played with other children who were white, there was an unspoken understanding of where I stood.

I experienced segregation and became accustomed to it. It was like the railroad tracks were the dividing line. On my side of the tracks, I had love and acceptance and community. Cross that bumpy line, and everything changed. On the other side, I felt discomfort, ridicule and confusion.

As I grew older, the difference in privilege became more apparent to me. I started asking questions about why some people were treated one way, and I was treated another. I knew I couldn't eat in the front of the restaurant, and I couldn't go to the restrooms or drinking fountains that were labeled "whites only."

I instinctively followed the rules and looked for signs that read "colored." The racism and segregation became increasingly more apparent as I reached high school, then college.

These experiences were based on the inescapable fact of the presence of the Ku Klux Klan (KKK). The KKK has always been so effective in what they do because their practices are based on fear. The images and association of the white hood and the burning stakes invoke terror.

I had quite a bit of experience with the KKK in college at Southern University in Baton Rouge. While marching across a bridge for a Martin Luther King demonstration, they were threatening to shoot us. People were also being arrested all around us simply for their peaceful acts of protest.

Fortunately, the KKK never came to our house when I was growing up in Gibsland, Louisiana. The closest experience I ever had with the Klan was when I was once approaching a railroad track on my bicycle with some friends. In the distance, we saw a group of guys driving towards us in a pick-up truck with a cross in the back.

My friends and I had to lay down on the ground in the hope they wouldn't see us. When they were clearly out of sight, we hopped back on our bikes and rode home as fast as we could. That was a chilling moment, and something that never leaves your memory.

Those were some tough times.

♪♪♪

One of my most significant racial confrontations happened during my college years back in my hometown of Gibsland. I was known in the community at the time for being part of the marching band at Southern University. I played percussion and received a full ride band scholarship. There had recently been a write-up about me in the paper, which caused tension with some people. On top of that, I never wore jeans; I always wore a nice suit and tie. My sister bought me my clothes, and I was never lacking in style.

I stopped to fill my car with gas at a station where my mom and sister had given their regular business for over 30 years. The owner of the service station had always been respectful of our family. We gave him a lot of gas sales over the years, so he appreciated that, and he knew us well.

I greeted the attendant on duty in my usual friendly demeanor. I could sense this guy had some issues with seeing a Black man in a suit and tie, and he was obviously not impressed. I went on about my business with what I was there to do; getting the car filled with gas, as I always would.

The following week, I was coming home by myself one night and drove up to our familiar gas station. The same guy was working as the attendant that evening. This was before the age of self-serve pumps, so I had no choice but to interact with him if I wanted to get gas.

"I just need two gallons," I said to him.

It became clear the unsettled feeling my appearance had given him the week prior had been building in him and had reached its boiling point.

There was a police officer who happened to be there at the same time, and he had struck up a conversation with me during the fill-up, asking me about my future plans. This officer had known and respected me and my family for quite some time. He knew I was not someone who would cause problems.

I had previously noticed there was a shotgun on a rack inside the station. The attendant was clearly becoming increasingly agitated, as I watched him go back inside. I could see he was reaching to take down the gun.

I sprang into self-preservation and survival mode. I knew as friendly and cordial as the officer had always been, I couldn't fully count on him for my protection. I sprinted to the entrance, dragged the startled attendant outside and beat him up before he could get a firm hand on the shotgun.

The officer was surprised and trying to process what had just happened, but he merely told me I needed to go home. I still believed he wanted to keep me from getting into trouble.

I drove back to the house, having an unsettled feeling of a calm before the storm. My mom was not at home at the time, and I was relieved to be alone since I sensed something was about to happen.

About an hour later, I heard the anticipated sound of cars approaching. Several police cars were quietly parking outside, surrounding our house. I was doing chores outside their line of vision, and I once again sprang into action. I got hold of my gun and quietly waited, hidden outside in a patch of trees by our shed. After what felt like an eternity of feeling my heart pounding in my chest, I watched the police cars drive away.

The next day, I went to talk to the gas station owner, who I trusted. I drove up under the gas station canopy and he knew something was definitely up when he saw the shotgun on the backseat and the pistol at my side.

I relayed to him what had happened the night before.

"I wanted to kill him," I told him frankly.

I knew it was time for me to leave Gibsland. With the racial climate, it had never been a safe place for me to be, even with the blissful innocence of growing up on my mother's farm. After leaving for college, Gibsland became an even more treacherous place for me.It was time to move to Shreveport. I had other dreams that I knew I had to fulfill.

It was time for me to spread my wings.

About six months later, I caught the bus for a rare visit back to Gibsland. The gas station was in the same location as the bus stop. This time, the gas station owner's father was there pumping the gas. As was my past habit, I asked him if I could use the phone to call my sister to come and pick me up.

"You didn't know this side of the station is for whites, and the side over there is for coloreds?" he asked in his slow deliberate drawl.

"I know there's a segregated restaurant, but I didn't think that applied to the gas station," I replied in disbelief.

Now I was angry. "Before I leave, I want to know how much our family owes so I can pay it off and never come back here again!"

He pretended like he couldn't find our credit slips. I took the box from him and found all our receipts. I wrote the check and stormed out.

I did not look back, and I never returned.

I told my sister about what had happened and what I had decided about discontinuing our business. She readily agreed with me.

Not long following that incident after returning on the bus herself, Minnie walked into the station to use the phone to call her husband, Bennie, to pick her up.

"Let me tell you about your baby brother," the owner's father said, preparing to launch into his version of the story, hoping she would view it all as a young angry Black man's "over-reaction."

Before he could say anymore, she politely confirmed that we would not be doing any business with him from that point forward and walked out the door.

Having principles, and following through on them, is vital.

♪♪♪

When Pat and I were living in Shreveport, every Saturday I would take my mother to her chiropractor in Waskom, Texas, about 25 miles away. One weekend, after her appointment, we stopped for a hamburger at a drive-in spot in Bossier City, Louisiana, just outside of Shreveport.

There was a trailer house set up to place food orders. We had a great time that day with no incidents, and the burgers were delicious. I knew I wanted to experience that food again.

It was only about a week later that my first child, Yolanda, was born. In the evening after leaving the hospital, I decided I would take Patsy's mother over to the same burger joint. When we parked, it was quiet and there were very few people around. I went over to the window at the front of the trailer and ordered our food.

I noticed there was a juke box inside and a young cat was sitting on a box beside it. The owner of the little restaurant was outside at the time. His wife was inside preparing food. I walked back to the car to wait for our food order, and I noticed a sign above another order window that read "colored." I hadn't seen that sign on my previous visit.

I went back up to the original window to pick up our food order. Just as I had paid, I looked up in time to see the same guy who had been inside sitting on the box coming towards me with a hammer in his hand.

"Can't you read?" were his first snide words.

"What are you talking about?" I asked. "What difference does it make?"

"It makes a lot of difference," he snarled.

That was it. He triggered me and I went off. I hit him in the face, and he dropped the hammer.

The owner of the spot ran inside yelling to his wife, "Get the gun, get the gun."

My mother-in-law sprang into action. She got out of the car, yelling at his wife to distract her, and stopped the woman from being able to grab the gun.

I really would have killed the hammer guy if he had threatened me any further. I was overcome with fury. When I was back in the car driving away, I actually attempted to run him over. I'm glad it turned out the way it did, and I did not end up harming the ignorant fool.

In those moments, I almost altered the course of my life. I was just so sick and tired of the blatant racism that was happening on a daily basis.

I think I knew at that time that I would not live in Louisiana forever, no matter how familiar it was. I was seeing firsthand what was happening in that social and political climate of the South.

I did keep that hammer for years as a reminder of that experience and the choices we make, for better or for worse, every minute of every day.

♩♩♪

"Racism is so universal in this country, so widespread, and deep-seated, that it is invisible because it is so normal." - **Shirley Chisholm**

Back in the day, African Americans went north thinking they had somehow arrived, finally escaping the perils of racism, only to find the similar experiences were still there.

People of color could move out of lower-class jobs, but the truth that they found was that it wasn't any different. It was hard to trust that an individual who was being acknowledged and patted on the back for a job well done wouldn't be called the N-word when they walked out the door. It was challenging to keep faith in any progress or perceived change.

In the country, our everyday experience of racism and discrimination was different. When I was a child growing up on a farm, and mainly being in town to pick up supplies or for an occasional appointment, we weren't aware of the racism constantly on the streets like the lived experience of an urban environment.

Living in the South presented blatant unfairness and bigotry.

The white sector conveyed to Blacks, "We live on this side of the tracks, you live on that side. And you had better stay over there!"

There were two different worlds that we lived in, with the lines of separation being very clear. I grew up in a segregated world, which did have its share of advantages.

The saying "It takes a village to raise a child" is true. In my generation, we had that village, and we had that support. We were united and we were together. And when we went to school, the teachers were in our corner. The people who were teaching us looked like us and had the same types of experiences that we had.

One of the biggest differences of today is that, in my generation, the opportunities and decisions were based in our community. We had quality leaders and we supported Black-owned businesses.

Because we did live in a more segregated Black community, those businesses were generally together geographically and easily accessible to the community. We had strong families and respected grandparents and elders. Most everybody worked together, and that was necessary for our livelihood and survival.

The struggle for civil rights with Dr. Martin Luther King, Jr. and many other activists, began our marching, demonstrations, and boycotts. Our voices grew louder, rightfully demanding justice and equality in our lives. However, even with the advantages that integration provided, the integrated change that resulted took away our values; it separated us and divided us as a race.

Our unity seemed to no longer be there. The type of inequality and integration that evolved helped to create a losing battle. The blurred lines, in my opinion, have created a lack and loss of community and identity. In the way it happened, integration was no more equal than segregation. Integration could ideally be a positive experience if everyone truly did receive equal treatment and resources.

School funding continues to be designated by zip code based on demographics. These targeted schools often struggle with a lack of technology and supplies, and they hire underqualified teachers who have no resemblance to the students who are underserved. These schools often close or fall victim to "school reform."

Schools became warehouses and holding tanks for the penitentiary. The school-to-prison pipeline is very real. Students are being "passed through" grade levels and, in turn, graduate unable to read or write. As a result, filling out a job application can be an impossibility.

White-controlled capitalism in our country effectively dictates where money is spent. After segregation was ruled unconstitutional, Black America had a seemingly wider range of options to spend its hard-earned dollars. In turn, Black-owned businesses were no longer as viable in the community.

The seeming freedoms and advantages of integration to further the success of African Americans soon became an apparent illusion. The Black worker is paid on Friday, often by a white employer. By Tuesday, a good part of that money is back in the hands of white capitalism.

The paycheck is spent paying the rent or mortgage to white landlords or bankers, buying goods and services from white-owned businesses, and going full circle back to lining the pockets of primarily white executives. Black-owned business is left unsupported due to convenience, franchise pricing, status, or name recognition; a reinforced belief system that the white businesses are somehow "better."

One of the biggest ongoing issues we continue to experience across the country is the lack of Black ownership, particularly in business. This I believe is in large part due to what is called the "Willie Lynch Syndrome."

In 1712, on the banks of the James River in Virginia, a slave owner named William Lynch allegedly gave a speech regarding the best method to control the enslaved individuals in the colony. The four-page letter, first printed in The St. Louis Black Pages' 1994 9th Anniversary Edition, is said to be a verbatim account of the speech given by Lynch.

The letter and speech are believed by many to be fictional due to some of the inaccuracies in the language of the day. However, it is a theory that took hold, and it makes a whole lot of sense – beyond the argument of whether the speech is factual or not.

The descriptive text is painfully difficult to read, as it instructs other slave owners on the "secret" to controlling Black enslaved people by setting them against each other.

The published words sum it up best as was written, in part:

"...I have a fool proof method for controlling your black slaves. I guarantee every one of you that if installed correctly it will control the slaves for at least 300 years...I use fear, distrust and envy for control purposes...I shall assure you that distrust is stronger than trust, and envy is stronger than adulation, respect or admiration...

"...The black slaves after receiving this indoctrination shall carry on and will become self-refueling and self-generating for hundreds of years, maybe thousands.

"Don't forget you must pitch the old black male vs. the young black male, and the young black male against the old black male. You must use the dark skin slaves vs. the light skin slaves, and the light skin slaves vs. the dark skin slaves. You must use the female vs. the male, and the male vs. the female. You must also have your white servants and overseers distrust all blacks, but it is necessary that your slaves trust and depend on us. They must love, respect and trust only us..."

Lynch believed that slave owners were employing the wrong

policy to achieve submission from their enslaved workers, and he had the philosophy that a hierarchy should be created in the enslaved community. Blacks at each level are then required to look up to people above them and are pitted against one another. Give them one year with this dysfunctional hierarchy and submission does not have to be taught, it just happens automatically.

Howard Denson, in 1993 publisher of the St. Louis Black Pages, accurately stated "Blacks still carry the negative mental legacy of slavery. I think we really need to address the things that hold us back. Blacks spend $400 million annually, but they believe they're poor and powerless because they've been conditioned to think that way."

The Willie Lynch speech may be an urban legend, but the concept of it holds a large degree of truth; enough truth that "Willie Lynch Syndrome" became a coined description. It stimulates a discussion about the psychic damage of slavery, and an understanding of a theory of what enslaved Black minds, as well as their bodies. It is often cited as a reason why Black people struggle to unite and find it so challenging to overcome centuries of institutional racism.

Blacks have been brainwashed to not be successful. The message is that one always has to look up to someone else. That's one of the main reasons we're dealing with this.

How do we change it? That's a tough question, with the many years of reinforcement that has been engrained in our psyches.

The principle of the Willie Lynch Syndrome says a lot about the former and current state of Black America. As an owner of a radio station, I had to deal with negativity and discrimination from advertisers – refusing to advertise with us or ignoring invoices, or the classic "Something's wrong with this invoice." I was reminded on a regular basis that color barriers and white economic power were, and still are, very real.

It's an ongoing challenge that people of color have to learn to fight, to deal with, and to overcome. And most importantly, continue to keep it moving, against all odds.

♪♪♪

Even though some things never seem to change, and racism is a foundational function of our culture, there have been some noticeable changes in certain areas of race relations.

Louisiana Tech is in Ruston, Louisiana, which is about a half hour from Gibsland. When I was a young boy, there was no way I could have even walked across that college campus. African Americans were not allowed to attend that university until well into the Civil Rights era.

Louisiana Tech opened as the Industrial Institute and College of Louisiana in 1894 during the Second Industrial Revolution. The original mission of the college was for the education of students in the arts and sciences for the purpose of developing an industrial economy in post-Reconstruction Louisiana.

Unfortunately, that mission did not include the inclusion of any African American students until 70 years later. Louisiana Tech, like most predominantly white institutions in the South, has a deep history of racial segregation.

During the mid-1960's, ninety percent of Black adults in Ruston had been barred from voting for decades. The White Citizen's Council maintained an active branch, espousing its policy of "massive resistance" to integration. Desegregating Louisiana Tech only happened under a federal court order.

In the spring of 1965, a brave young man and native of Quitman, Louisiana, by the name of James Earl Potts transferred from Grambling College upon his admittance to Louisiana Polytechnic Institute (now Louisiana Tech).

A few months later, Bertha Bradford, a young courageous woman and native of Jonesboro, Louisiana, came to the Institute in Ruston. These first two Black students, with their unparalleled strength, affected change and blazed a challenging trail for the future of the integration of Louisiana Tech.

That fall, 28 Black students enrolled at the school. By 1968, African American students were finally represented in every department on the campus.

In 2016, Louisiana Tech University and its Office of Multicultural Affairs created a scholarship to honor the legacy of James Earl Potts and Bertha Bradford-Robinson. The annual scholarship supports educational opportunities for minority students attending Louisiana Tech and is intended to enrich the cultural and diversity experiences of the university's campus community.

Years later when I was home for a visit, I went to see my cousin's son, Kevin Lewis, play basketball at Louisiana Tech. I was very reflective when I walked inside that gymnasium and saw folks of all races having a good time. The feelings went very deep for me, watching the diversity on the team, playing basketball together.

I looked around at families of all colors hollering and screaming, cheering for the students, no matter their ethnicity. There was such a significant contrast in that moment. It brought tears to my eyes.

We are making progress, even if it seems slow, or even nonexistent at times.

20 | God's Role in My Life

"Faith is taking the first step even when you can't see the whole staircase."
- **Dr. Martin Luther King, Jr.**

I grew up in a religious family, with my mother at its center. She was very much a churchgoing, loving, giving and caring person, a true Christian in every sense of the word.

In turn, my entire life has been shaped by religion. As long as I can remember, from the time I was five or six years old, I would be in church almost every Sunday, as well as at Bible Study. I would also go to what is now called Vacation Bible School, which was like a summer camp. My childhood was very religion-centered.

As a young adult, I moved away from religion and attending church, which I know is not uncommon for many people at that stage in their lives. When I left for college, I participated in the often-customary drinking and partying. My focus shifted to the new world of leaving home.

As time marched on, I continued towards a different circuit of life, and distractions kept me from my prior faithful church attendance and the recognized importance of God in my life. I drifted off that course and I didn't belong to a church anymore.

This carried over into my middle adulthood. Life was fast when

I was introduced to the music industry. I believed that I knew it all, and I felt I didn't need the influence of a higher power.

And even though I wasn't involved in religion for a lengthy span of my life, there was still a foundational part of me, deep in my soul, that continued to understand the wisdom and knowledge of spirituality. I didn't ever forget it – although I acted like I had at times.

Having been brought up in a religious household, surrounded by people who loved me, and always being exposed to a teaching process of what the bible is about, gave me the foundation of following God's will. That part became rooted in my being and even as I strayed, I was able to find my way back when I was finally ready.

When my mom and my brother passed so close together, only seven months apart, I was incredibly angry with God. That was the height of my distancing from religion. I didn't feel like I could ever go back into a relationship with a God who would take the people I love away from me in an instant. It felt like the cruelest thing imaginable, without being able to even comprehend one loss before the other happened so unexpectedly as well.

I give thanks to my young son who gave me the gift of his wisdom when I needed it most so long ago, walking along the railroad tracks while pheasant hunting. That was the turning point for me of beginning to find my way back to a healthy relationship with God. A God who would never leave me alone in a time of need or give me any more than I can ever handle.

♪♪♪

Patsy also came from a religious family and she ultimately became the backbone of my involvement in church and religious activities.

She was a great influence on so many parts of my life, and she often knew what I needed more than I did.

Upon our move to Denver, my wife and my children continued their faithful church-going tradition. Patsy and the kids joined Mount Gilead Baptist Church where the Reverend Acen Phillips was the pastor.

On Sundays, Patsy would regularly ask me if I wanted to go to church with the family.

"Nah, y'all go ahead," was my standard reply.

I just didn't feel like I was ready to attend. The irony of it was Reverend Phillips was a very close friend of mine. I had interviewed him numerous times on KDKO, and our friendship tie continued to strengthen.

He considered me to be a part of his church, and for years he would proudly proclaim to people, "Daddio and his family are members of my church."

This always made me feel good and I was proud to be thought of as a part of Reverend Phillips' church. I had such a high regard for him as well.

♪♪♪

After I took over KDKO, I began to have Gospel Sundays on the radio. One Sunday, my sister in Louisiana happened to listen and she found out some news that sparked a chord in her.

The next time I was in my hometown visiting, Minnie made the comment to me, "Y'all have taken our pastor from our church."

I was puzzled and asked her what she meant. By that time, my immediate family in Denver had moved over to Central Baptist Church, a historic church in Five Points. Minnie proceeded to tell me their pastor had left and moved to Denver. His name was Reverend Willie Simmons.

The name didn't register at the time. Because I wasn't yet joining my family at church, I hadn't connected who he was.

I belonged to Temple Light Social Club in Denver. After my return from Gibsland, in a conversation with our club president, I learned we had a member whose name was Simmons. She made the comment that Mr. Simmons' cousin came here from Monroe, Louisiana, and was now a pastor at Central Baptist Church.

It still went in one ear and out the other.

My message from God to connect with this man only continued to get stronger. A short while after that, when we were having our annual Juneteenth celebration in Denver, a woman approached me and inquired if I was from Gibsland, Louisiana.

"Well, yes," I replied, surprised to hear someone ask about my small hometown. "What do you know about Gibsland?"

"My husband was a pastor at a church there and he's been trying to catch up with you. Have you heard of Reverend Simmons?" she asked. "He is right up there on stage now, and a part of the program that's about to start."

She pointed him out to me, and in that same moment he waved to me as he saw me having a conversation with his wife.

The following Monday morning he was in my office.

Thanks to the persistence of my wife and daughters, my relationship to a church family was about to take a turn, and I had no idea what a positive shift my life would experience.

♪♪♪

Every Sunday morning, I would get up and shine my shoes. Shoes all over the floor. This has been a favorite ritual of mine throughout most of my life. I love to shine shoes.

One Sunday, my wife and our youngest daughter, Jasmine, were getting ready for church. Our daughter, Yolanda, called to confirm they were meeting for the service at Central Baptist Church. I had answered the phone and before I turned it over to my wife, Yolanda invited me to go along - as had become everyone's usual ritual.

And as expected, I declined.

"I'll go another time," I told Patsy as she got off the call.

As I headed up the stairs, something I couldn't explain just told me I should go to church. It was one of those intuitive revelations that I had come to recognize and welcome. I came back downstairs dressed and ready to go. It really shocked my wife and daughter. I was all set, and I was not going to wait on nobody.

The three of us drove to Central Baptist to meet Yolanda. The church has its own amazing history. It is the second oldest African American church in Denver, now over 130 years old in the heart of Five Points. The oldest, Zion Baptist Church was established in Five Points in 1863. Central Baptist Church, built behind where the Blair-Caldwell African American Research Library is now located, was organized in the fall of 1891 with 30 members.

After we parked and were walking up to the church, the sanctuary windows were open, and I heard singing and welcoming praise. The familiar sound created a comforting association of the days of my childhood. We entered and I saw the church was packed.

There were only four seats available in the back of the church.

Yolanda, Jasmine, Patsy and I filed in and savored our Sunday morning worship, unabashedly giving thanks to God in His Glory. I felt lighter in my whole being and returned the next Sunday.

Even though now I was rushing to get there, this week there were only three seats left in the back of the church and one seat in the very front. My wife and daughters settled into the back three seats, and the usher led me up to the front of the church and seated me in that front seat next to the deacons.

The following Sunday, it was the same situation. That front seat had become my own, and it seemed to be part of a Divine plan.

I can't explain what happened that third Sunday after the service was over. It was another one of those intuitive moments that was guiding me. The next thing I knew I was shaking Reverend Simmons' hand and I made plans to officially join the church.

I was there as a faithful member of Central Baptist, active and dedicated along with my wife, for the next 20 years. I became a deacon and was now a true churchgoer again. I was a part of accomplishing great things as a church over the course of those two decades.

♪♪♪

Around the same time I began attending church regularly again, I became very in tune to the miracles of God at work in my life on a daily basis. I hadn't been aware of that for a while.

I realized the signs and subtle messages had been there all along, but I was too self-absorbed to truly pay attention. I began to marvel at the trials and tribulations – the challenges and triumphs - that God had carried me through. I realized the things I had faced would have been insurmountable without His love and guidance.

After a half-century of life, I really started looking at the little things, and all the indicators that had always been there. God never gave up on me, which helped me to never give up on myself, or my dreams, no matter how rocky the road, or winding the path.

There were examples of the Lord's sometimes subtle messages that really stand out in my memory.

One time when I went home to Louisiana, my sister had some remodeling done on her house. It was back in the day when the boxy window air conditioners were the primary form of cooling indoor air.

When I arrived, Minnie greeted me and said, "I've got a problem. I want you to come and look at the back room where I put the AC in. It's not stable," she continued. "I had to get a carpenter to come in, but it still isn't right. I'd like for you to secure that in the next couple days."

I went to the lumber company and bought what I needed. I put the tools and wood by the window and then got distracted by so many other events going on, I forgot all about it. When I was almost ready to leave, I remembered I hadn't fixed the window.

All the measurements I had put together were just right, but it was a window with a screen so when the air conditioner was installed, it stuck out a little bit. The frame I put in wouldn't fit with the screen.

I thought, "Oh man, I have to take the whole thing out and restructure it another way."

It was off to the hardware store to pick up a handsaw that I discovered I needed. As I started out, I saw my friend's truck at his house down the street. He was living in their family home and his brother had a house right next door to him. I decided I would stop in to say hi since I was driving by.

When I drove up, I heard the distinctive sound of an electric saw in the backyard of his brother's house. As we exchanged greetings, I asked about the saw that I had heard. It turns out it was his wife using the saw; she built patio furniture.

I said to my friend, "I am wondering if she'll let me use the saw to cut the boards I need."

I proceeded into the backyard to ask his wife. She told me the lumber along the fence was available for whatever I needed. I found a few pieces that would work well, and I got them cut to the right size.

Driving back up the street to my sister's home in reflection, I was marveling that here I had been looking for a hand saw, and an electric saw appeared for me.

When I arrived back at the house, I told Pat and Minnie in wonderment, "Guess what happened?"

I finished the air conditioning project, to the gratitude of my sister, and then Pat and I were on our way back home.

I continue to discern the role Divine Intervention plays in my life. The more I pay attention, the more it seems to become even more apparent.

♪♪♪

Some unfortunate controversy came up with Reverend Simmons after his nearly 20 years of service to the church. The board, with agreement from much of the congregation, decided to let him go after he had built a million-dollar church. My thought was getting rid of this man makes no kind of sense, but they were insistent, and they let him go.

I walked out with him the night he resigned, along with several other members, a few of the other deacons and his brother. After his years of service and the level I thought he had brought the church, I wasn't ready to leave his side and wanted to continue my support of him. I had to step away from Central Baptist for a while.

I got a call from Reverend Simmons while I was visiting in Louisiana. He told me he was thinking about starting another church. After I got back home, we met at one of the members' homes with about 50 other people to discuss this vision. We all supported the idea of the new church, and New Relationship Baptist was formed.

After the one-year anniversary and a big celebration of the church's success, Reverend Simmons decided he wanted to do a travelling ministry. His desire was to have a Sunday service in Denver one week, then the next week a service in California, and the following week a service in Louisiana.

I objected to that very much because in my opinion, that would never work. What would his local parishioners do on those off Sundays? I made up my mind that I couldn't go along with this plan, and therefore I couldn't stay.

As a footnote, I continue to have a great deal of respect for Reverend Simmons, and we remain close. He officiated Patsy's funeral service in Louisiana, and Reverend DeWayne Moore, another very influential pastor in my life, led the beautiful memorial service here in Denver.

♪♪♪

I was back to not having a church to call my own and was waiting for God to lead me to where I was meant to be. I had a close friend named Carlos Houston who, along with his wife, Ruby, also belonged to Temple Light Social Club. Carlos was a deacon, a lead singer in the choir, and an active member at Macedonia Baptist Church. Sadly, he passed away.

Fate and faith always have a way of stepping in and showing up at just the right time. When I attended Carlos' funeral at Macedonia Baptist Church, I was very impressed with the pastor who conducted the service. Patsy and I sat with the family, and this pastor, Reverend DeWayne Moore, came over to share his condolences with the family and shook my hand.

I had learned that the church had been looking for a pastor for several years. I asked Ruby if Reverend Moore had been selected as the church's senior pastor. She said no, they were still looking for somebody. I was surprised that he had not been chosen to have a permanent and higher role in their congregation based on how dynamic he had been in his message.

I had promoted him on KDKO when he began preaching in Denver, but I had never been to the church to hear him. After the funeral service, I complimented and congratulated Pastor Moore on the message he had delivered. I expressed that I was impressed and was happy to finally have an opportunity to share in his Word for the first time.

I proceeded to tell him if he ever wanted to start his own church, I would wholeheartedly support him and be a part of his new venture.

As I exited and told him farewell in the doorway, I reminded him again, "If you decide to leave this church, or wherever you end up going, I will follow."

He appreciated my expression of gratitude, and we exchanged phone numbers.

A few months later, Pastor Moore called me at the office to tell me that he had made up his mind, and he was planning to start that church.

"When is this going to happen?" I asked him.

"This coming Sunday," was his reply.

That Sunday, my wife and I drove over to the first-time worship location of Ebenezer Baptist Church in Aurora. There were so many cars, we couldn't find a parking place anywhere close by.

There were 326 people in attendance that first Sunday. They even had to open the dividing wall of the Summit building. The next Sunday was the same situation - they ended up opening another wall and there were people as far as you could see. After the third Sunday, the people in charge of the building said they couldn't accommodate us anymore because of the exponential growth of the newly developed church.

After that, we were able to hold services over at the Double Tree Hotel with 200 to 300 people in attendance each Sunday. My wife and I became faithful members at this newly established church, and I became an active deacon.

On October 20, 2012, Ebenezer Baptist Church was admitted into the Northern District Baptist Association at the Morning Star Baptist Church led by the moderator Pastor Hardy D. Swazer.

On November 10, 2012, at New Hope Baptist Church in Pueblo, Colorado, it was moved by Bishop Acen Phillips, Pastor of New Birth Temple of Praise Church of Denver and seconded by Pastor James Dotson of Trinity Baptist Church of Colorado Springs, that Ebenezer Baptist Church be accepted as a member of the Western States Baptist Convention. The vote was unanimous and approved by President Frank M. Davis.

In March of 2013, we officially installed Reverend DeWayne Moore as our Founding Senior Pastor.

At this writing, the services are being held at the Park Hill Seventh Day Adventist Church in Denver. Since the Seventh Day Adventists have their services on Saturdays, Ebenezer Baptist can hold its service Sunday.

♪♪♪

Even though I didn't initially attend church very often after both Minnie and Patsy passed, it was very different from when I lost my mother and brother. The anger is not there. My soul is very much at peace, and I have a continuing important relationship with God.

I've dedicated my life to serving God and my community. I have valued being involved in various organizations, assisting in any way I can as a part of my deeply rooted Christianity. I ask God every day to keep me strong so I can continue my service to humankind.

I know there's a God. I don't just believe; I know because of the wonderful things He has done for me. I encourage anyone anytime I have a chance to give help and service in this world.

GOD IS GREAT! His role in my life has been an amazing gift to me. He has brought me through many ups and downs, and hardships. All I can say is to pass it on. I try to help other people every day. I know that's what God has put me here to do, and my goal is to do just that with purpose and determination.

It took me some time to get there on my winding journey, but my destination has rewarded me beyond measure. My spiritual self has grown very much over the years, and I thank God each day for all His gifts and guidance in my life.

21 | Motivation

ııl|ıı||ıı|ı 🎤 ıı|ıı||ıı||ı

> "If you can't fly then run, if you can't run then walk, if you can't walk then crawl, but whatever you do you have to keep moving forward."
>
> **- Dr. Martin Luther King, Jr.**

One of the primary messages I give to others is to try and do something with your life, even if it's just opening a door or saying good morning. I make a point to model this behavior for everyone each day.

People don't realize what a simple "good morning" means. Or even just a smile. People go to the doctor's office and sit there without saying a word to anyone.

Talk to people. Don't be so depressed.

I was at Cherry Creek Reservoir one day last year. A guy drove up and got out of the car with his fishing pole. This may not seem extraordinary, until I tell you this man had no legs.

I thought about the challenges he must face every day in doing what may seem for most of us the simplest of things. It should give us pause to not take for granted the tasks that we each don't even think about in the precious moments of our lives that become automated and routine.

I said to myself, "What are you crying about?"

So, your back is hurting. Stop pitying yourself. Lots of people don't feel like getting up in the morning, and they overcome their own adversities with trust and faith. If we could think about it that way, I believe life would be much better.

I'll walk onto an elevator and in my voice as it is, strong and booming, I'll say "Good morning!"

People usually act like they don't even see me.

Have you noticed how almost everyone will intently stare at the numbers indicating which floor is approaching? Or some may look down at the floor or check their mobile devices as a welcome distraction rather than interacting with another person.

Acknowledging and speaking to others, no matter where we are, is what I think everyone should do. And we should always speak out for what we think is right. I have never been afraid to talk about anything, and tell it like it is

I believe there's something good in everybody. Even the individuals who we see as doing evil to us, there's good in them too. We need to stop looking at just the bad. I have always been a strong proponent of giving back to the community and I do my best to perform random acts of kindness each and every day. I believe that God commands us to do so by passing a blessing on to others.

♪♪♪

When I was training people at KDKO, I would try to teach every aspect of the job and each part of the station. When someone came to work, they didn't have to be just an announcer or a programmer playing music. The door would be open for them to become a traffic director, a music director, a program director, or ultimately an owner.

I wanted to try to teach them every part of the business, so they could be independent when they moved on from KDKO.

I wanted my employees to understand everything from copyrighting to programming, because all of this gives each individual some opportunity. Teaching ownership was so important as a reminder that anyone can go much further than being an employee of someone else. I wanted them to be independent when they left and feel inspired to continue pursuing their own dreams and purpose. One of the biggest reasons I went into the radio business was to help other people of color gain employment in broadcasting.

It's not an easy door to open.

♪♪♪

I have always had a commitment to be successful and I have had unique life experiences that I believe can impact other people's lives in positive ways. I have never done anything just for the sake of doing it. I believe it is always important to be genuine and to be uniquely who you are.

I often would ask myself in the early days before I owned KDKO, "If I could actually do this, how would it happen being a Black man?"

When I was the only Black radio station owner from the West Coast to Kansas City, Missouri. I would ask myself, "What would be the reason? What was the reason?"

My personal answer then and now is always the same. God.

God is the One who makes things happen. In my view, He is the One who guides us towards the decisions that we are supposed to make, the One who directs us as to how we are meant to live each day.

It has become increasingly clear to me how our paths are laid out according to God's plan for each of us. We, as humans, have a tendency to want to deal with everyday problems we encounter, big and small, all by ourselves. We want to make everything an "I" situation, and it's not. God put each one of us here for a specific purpose. Many people live their entire lives never understanding what their purpose is – never taking the initiative or making the effort to figure it out. And although God is at the helm of our ship, I also believe that we must be co-creators of our own destinies. We can't just sit back and wait for something to happen; we must take an active role if we want to accomplish our goals.

It is a process that takes patience. To be able to reap the true benefits of a vision or a dream, one needs to sit back and observe; take notes. When I was working at the various radio stations that were stepping-stones to my success, I carried a little black book. And every day, with great thought, I wrote down the problems that the owner of the station was having.

In turn, I developed a clear picture of how to handle and find solutions to those issues for when I would one day encounter the same problems as a radio station owner myself. I felt more prepared to put out the everyday fires of life.

I came to Denver 56 years ago with a dream and a vision to own a Black radio station. There was a big market in Houston and yet Denver was the destined location, where I didn't know a single soul. It was so important to me to open the door of opportunity for others.

After years of hard work, that dream and well-thought-out vision, became a reality. I'm a fighter, and a person who is determined to win.

If someone were to ask me what motivated me during that time, what kept me going, what contributed to my success, I would have to say it was my belief in myself and my ability to realize my dreams. If you have an idea or a conviction, stick with it, no matter what anyone else tells you or believes.

I know from experience what it is like to have someone put forward negative thoughts about a personal dream. If you allow this influence to take hold in your mind or soul, it can destroy your potential for success.

Back in the day when I first started sharing my dream with my sister about my desire to own a radio station, as supportive as she was of me, I saw my words go in one ear and out the other. Minnie finally asked me to stop talking about it, and I did – at least around her. But I never stopped believing that I was one day going to accomplish this unheard-of feat.

I continued to hear my mother's words: "You can accomplish anything as long as you just never give up."

After my dream became a reality, my sister apologized and acknowledged my persistence.

"I want to congratulate you," she said. "I want to give you all the credit in the world because you never gave up."

♪♪♪

Our world is controlled so often by fear. People who care about you may be trying to protect you from perceived failure, or the ingrained limitations that have been imposed on us by the majority culture. It is vital to understand that not ever giving up is vitally important to any present or future success.

Holding on to your personal dreams and goals, through thick and thin, is essential. I can tell you that it is not going to be easy. There are racial barriers and there are hardships that need to be dealt with on a daily basis.

I've heard the quote that life is only 10% what happens to us, and 90% how we deal with it, and that is so true. A winning attitude overcame many obstacles which had tried to block my path.

I thank the many individuals who presented me with opportunities to bring me closer to my goals. These opportunities were not always apparent or obvious, and I had to always have my eyes open and stay in tune with my awareness in order to recognize and seize the often-subtle processes and steps along the way.

As Muhmmad Ali would say, "Keep your eye on the prize."

Most importantly, let God guide you. Always have faith. Believe in yourself, and others will believe in you too.

22 | Capturing History and Stories

"Every day, men and women become legends."

- Common

So many musicians have been forgotten over the years. Number one hits of the past have faded from people's memories. It is a tragedy to lose those memories and the music of so much amazing talent.

It is similar with the narratives of people of all walks of life who have shaped our world, the legends and the lesser knowns. Everyone has an incredible story that is so often lost in our shortened attention spans and fast-paced culture, filled with micro-sound bites and interesting blurbs of the day spread for fleeting moments across social media.

It is more vital than ever that these legacies and life stories are honored and re-told for those who choose to listen. Even those performers who remain in the forefront have aspects of their stories that may surprise us.

I send out the challenge to everyone to explore the history of these artists, whether your favorite, or someone you just heard about, and to take the opportunity to learn a unique aspect of the individual's personality or experiences. Listen to a few of their songs; their music, their lyrics, and their message.

You might discover something that could inspire your own life.

♪♪♪

Jack the Rapper was the father of Black radio and someone who inspired my life. I am very grateful to him for opening doors in the radio industry. I had the opportunity to bring him to Denver in the early 80s. It was important to share with people the man who made it possible for me to pursue my radio dream.

His given name was Joseph Deighton Gibson, Jr. and he was born in Chicago, Illinois in 1920. In 1949, he started the first Black-owned and operated radio station in the U.S. – Atlanta's WERD. A long-time radio icon in the 1950s, he starred in the first radio soap opera to feature an all-Black cast, entitled *Here Comes Tomorrow*. He was initially known as Jockey Jack in the radio world, before becoming Jack the Rapper.

He was the first National Director of Promotions and Public Relations for Motown Records, joining the staff in 1963 where he mentored artists such as The Jackson Five, Marvin Gaye, The Supremes and Stevie Wonder.

Jack the Rapper founded an organization for Black DJs called NARA (National Association of Radio Announcers). He created a newsletter that became the first Black music trade magazine, *Mello Yello*, reflecting the color of the stock of paper he used to stand out from his competitors. He earned his greatest notoriety for his annual Black radio convention, "Jack the Rapper Family Affair," that began in 1977

Jack the Rapper died in January 2000 at the age of 79, leaving an incredible legacy.

♪♪♪

Berry Gordy, Jr. dropped out of high school to pursue his dream of becoming a professional boxer. The Korean War draft disrupted this dream. Upon returning from the war, Gordy opened a music store in Detroit to pursue his other passion, but the business failed.

He married and began to follow a traditional Detroit path working in the auto industry. Unable to escape his love of music, Berry began writing and recording songs with a young artist named Jackie Wilson. His first success as a songwriter was with Jackie Wilson's 1957 hit "Reet Petite."

Fueling a renewed dream, Gordy received an $800 loan from his father in 1959. And that's how Motown was born.

In 1966, Berry Gordy refused to sign The Jackson 5, because he didn't want to work with any more children. A year later, Gladys Knight is the one who convinced him to change his mind.

So many artists benefitted from Gordy's songwriting skills and Motown label including Smokey Robinson and the Miracles, the Supremes, the Four Tops, the Temptations, Gladys Knight and the Pips, the Jackson 5, Mary Wells, Stevie Wonder, Marvin Gaye, among others. Motown's success also depended on other collaborative songwriters such as Eddie Holland, Lamont Dozier, and Brian Holland.

In 2013, Mr. Gordy became the first living person to receive the Songwriter's Hall of Fame's Pioneer Award.

♪♪♪

Marvin Pentz Gaye, Jr. expressed that his greatest influence growing up was Marvin, Sr., even though his preacher father beat him often from the time he was seven years old into his teenage years. His rebellion against all authority distanced him from his father as he chose a different path from ministry.

Marvin dropped out of high school to join the Air Force. This was short-lived as he had little tolerance for the discipline or the menial tasks. As he grew older, Marvin was very inspired by segments of the mission of the Black Panther Party, particularly their efforts to provide free meals to families in need.

A songwriter who always advocated social change through non-violence, Marvin had a four-octave vocal range and played piano, keyboard, synthesizer, and organ, along with a number of percussion instruments. His Motown career spanned two decades.

In 1963, Marvin married Berry Gordy's sister, Anna Gordy. They remained together for a decade.

On April 1, 1984, Marvin Gaye's life came to a tragic end when he intervened in a fight between his parents the day before his 45th birthday. A physical altercation ensued between he and his father. Marvin Gay, Sr. ended up shooting his son twice, one being a bullet to his heart – with a pistol that Marvin had allegedly bought for his father to defend himself from potential intruders. His father's sentence was reduced following a diagnosis of a brain tumor.

♪♪♪

Atlanta native Gladys Knight sang regularly in the church choir as she was growing up. At the age of eight, she, along with her brother, sister, and two cousins spontaneously performed at her brother's 10th birthday party. Her mother encouraged them to continue to perform as a group, initially calling them "The Little Knight Group,"

Their first official gig was an afternoon social at the YWCA, earning ten dollars. They soon decided to name themselves "The Pips," inspired by the nickname of another cousin, James "Pip" Woods.

Over the next several years, the young Pips performed in local talent shows, winning each one. This led to a record contract and their fame accelerated from there. The group debuted their first album in 1960.

When she was 22 in 1966, Gladys Knight and the Pips joined the Motown Records family after they had moved to Detroit. Gladys was hesitant to sign the contract but was outvoted by her group. In their early days with Motown, they toured as the opening act for The Supremes.

After leaving Motown seven years later, Gladys Knight and the Pips gained even greater success as they were overshadowing other Motown singers. In the late 80s, Gladys exclusively focused on her solo career.

In 1996, she was inducted into the Rock and Roll Hall of Fame and had received a star on the Hollywood Walk of Fame. The Empress of Soul is also included in the Rolling Stone's list of the Greatest Singers of All Time, and she has won seven Grammy awards.

♪♪♪

The Supremes were the most well-known and successful female Motown group, even rivaling the Beatles in their popularity. Originating in Detroit in 1959 as The Primettes, the group was originally created as a sister act to The Primes (with Paul Williams and Eddie Kendricks, who went on to form the Temptations).

Diana Ross, Florence Ballard, Betty McGloan, and Mary Wilson were teenagers from the Brewster-Douglas Public Housing Project at their start. Smokey Robinson helped these young women get their audition at Motown, and Berry Gordy originally wanted them to finish high school before signing them to a contract. The determined teens did not want to wait and would not give up, providing back-up hand claps to other Motown artists. They eventually convinced Gordy, who relented and signed them in January of 1961. He gave them a list of names to choose from, among them "The Darleens," "The Sweet P's", "The Melodees," "The Royaltones," and "The Jewelettes." Florence Ballard decided on "The Supremes," and the rest is history.

Barbara Martin replaced McGloan in 1960, leaving herself in 1962. Diana Ross left the group in 1970 to pursue her solo career and was replaced by Jean Terell. The group members changed frequently after 1972, and The Supremes disbanded in 1977, after 18 years of stardom.

♪♪♪

The Temptations (originally called the Elgins when they formed in Detroit in 1960) were named the Greatest Rhythm and Blues Artists of all time by *Billboard* Magazine. They had sixteen number one albums and fourteen number one hit singles. The Temptations were initially considered "no hit wonders" as they had seven different singles before having their first charting single in 1964; "The Way You Do the Things You Do." That same year, "My Girl," topped the charts at number one.

This iconic group had the second longest run with Motown at 40 years (Stevie Wonder had the longest tenure at nearly 60 years). They were the first Motown group to win a Grammy award in 1969 for their ninth studio album, *Cloud Nine*.

The Temptations are now celebrating over 60 years of music. They are currently in the midst of an International Tour. Their last album was released in 2022, *Temptations 60*.

At the time of this writing, Otis Williams, at the age of 81, is the surviving founding member of the original group, and continues to perform.

♪♪♪

B.B. King was a blues singer, songwriter, guitarist and record producer, founding his own record label, Blues Boys Kingdom. He performed on average at more than 200 concerts per year into his 70s. His record year for appearances was 342 in 1956.

Riley B. King was born in Mississippi to Sharecropper parents in 1925. He sang in a gospel choir when he was a young boy and was forbidden by his mother to play the blues as she considered it to be anti-religious. When he was 18, King left the town where he grew up to be a tractor driver and play guitar with a gospel group.

As a young man, he hosted a blue's show on a radio station, WDHI, in Memphis. There he earned the nickname "Beale Street Blues Boy" which was shortened to "Blues Boy" and the root of "B.B."

Mr. King became one of the most important names in the R&B scene in the 1950s after his first *Billboard* R&B charted number one hit "3 O'clock Blues," leading to an increase in his earnings from $85 a week to $2500.

He earned his first of fifteen Grammy Awards in 1971 for his song "The Thrill is Gone." The prolific artist released more than 50 albums with his messages of universal hope, love, peace and joy.

B.B. became a licensed pilot at 38 and often flew himself to gigs until the age of 70. He performed at Red Rocks when he was over 80 years old.

A strong proponent of prison reform, he co-founded the Foundation for the Advancement of Inmate Rehabilitation and Recreation.

B.B. said, "There are so many sounds I still want to make, so many things I haven't yet done."

He certainly accomplished a lot and left behind an amazing legacy when he passed in 2015 at the age of 89.

♪♪♪

James Joseph Brown began his life with next to nothing. Almost stillborn in 1933, to a 16-year-old mother and a 21-year-old father, inside a South Carolina shack without windows, electricity, gas or running water, James had to start out early working hard just to survive.

His mother left when he was four years old in order to escape his abusive father. A few years later, James went to live with his aunt in her brothel in Augusta, Georgia. He was often beaten by his father and other male tenants. James learned to tap dance and became self-taught in playing guitar, piano and harmonica. This earned him some spare change from the stationed troops at the start of World War II and gained his aunt some clients.

In seventh grade, the impoverished child was sent home from school for having "insufficient clothes" and never went back.

As a teen, James had a brief career as a boxer and had a passion for baseball as well, both of which he would have liked to have pursued at a deeper level.

At 16, the young hustler was convicted of robbery and sentenced to the Georgia Juvenile Training Institute. Inside the detention center, he formed a gospel quartet with three of his cellmates.

R&B musician and talent scout Bobby Byrd discovered James' talent while visiting the prison. He vouched for him and ensured his early parole after a shortened sentence of three years. One of the court stipulations was that Brown would "sing for the Lord."

Mr. Dynamite's success skyrocketed in the mid-1950s as lead singer of his R&B group founded by Bobby Byrd, the Famous Flames with the James Brown Band. Their well-known hit singles were "Please, Please, Please" and "Try Me."

His notoriety peaked in the 1960s with his live album *Live at the Apollo* and hit singles "I Feel Good" and "It's a Man's Man's Man's World." By the late 1960s, Soul Brother No. 1 had evolved from a blues and gospel-based style into an originator of funk music.

The performances of the Godfather of Soul were famous for their intensity and length. His self-stated intent was to "give people more than what they came for." James demanded extreme discipline, perfection, and precision from his musicians and dancers. Infractions would result in fines paid by his band members.

The artist recorded an impressive 17 singles that reached number one on the *Billboard* R&B charts, as well as holding the record for the most singles listed on the *Billboard* Hot 100 chart. He was very passionate about the importance of education and wrote songs and advocated towards this goal.

The day after Martin Luther King, Jr. was assassinated on April 5, 1968, in Memphis, James performed a free citywide televised concert at the Boston Garden to maintain public order and help the community.

The Hardest Working Man in Show Business who did vocals, keyboard, harmonica, drums and guitar was one of the first ten inductees into the Rock and Roll Hall of Fame at its inaugural induction in New York in 1986. He was posthumously inducted into the first class of the Rhythm and Blues Music Hall of Fame in 2013 as an artist and then in 2017 as a songwriter.

A week before he died, James gave out toys and turkeys for Christmas dinners to children at an Atlanta orphanage, even though his health was failing at the time.

On December 25, 2006, James Brown left his legacy as a great gift to the world, when he passed from complications of pneumonia at the age of 73.

Rest in Peace, my brother.

♪♪♪

In addition to artists and musicians, there are radio stations around the country that have very interesting stories. It's important to recognize their contributions to the radio industry and the existence and firsts of the African Americans who were a part of that history.

WLAC in Nashville, first signed on the air in 1926. The call letters were chosen to contain an acronym for the first owner of the station, the Life and Casualty Insurance Company of Tennessee.

WLAC became known as the radio station where country music essentially first developed and the source where it became a national phenomenon. Just as the format shifted from country to R&B with KDKO, WLAC's Black music format was introduced after World War II, when the disc jockey Gene Nobles of the "Dance Hour Show" began getting mail requests from veterans who had been exposed to the early roots of R&B.

Later, in response to the contention that African Americans in rural areas of the South were still underserved by radio, the FCC granted WLAC permission to have one of the strongest signals in the country, provided that the station broadcast rhythm and blues.

In the 50s, 60s, and 70s, WLAC was legendary for its nighttime R&B. Thanks to the station's clear channel designation, particularly after dark, the signal reached most of the Eastern and Midwestern United States. WLAC described itself as the nighttime station for half the nation. Several foreign countries, particularly islands in the Caribbean and southern Canada were within range of the station's nocturnal signal.

In the late 60s, the sale's manager at WLAC sought to hire Don Whitehead, the nation's first Black news radio broadcaster employed by a major white owned radio station. He traveled around WLAC's listening area promoting Historically Black Colleges & Universities (HBCUs) and played a major role in increasing the enrollment of African Americans attending college.

In another format change, WLAC has been branded Talkradio 98.3 &1510 since 1980.

An interesting fact about radio has to do with the number of watts designated for different stations. The level of watts refers to the transmitter output, and not how much it takes to power the transmitter and run all the equipment.

There were rules and regulations set in place to protect the signals of specific stations. These requirements were strictly enforced, and other stations could be penalized with a hefty fine if they didn't respect these guidelines. The high-powered stations had to cut back at sunset until sunrise to protect specified radio stations around the country. KOA was one of those protected stations in Colorado.

WLAC in Nashville was another station signal that we had to

respect, and "bow down" to, so to speak. KDKO was considered a daytime station. We were required to drop from 10,000 watts to 5,000 watts at sunset. Our transmission went from a circle configuration during the day to a figure eight when it got dark. Aurora was at the center of that figure eight, so people there would often say at night, "We can't hear you."

We were strictly regulated and didn't have a choice in our level of output. The powers that be would measure the number of watts coming from each separate radio station. If you went outside your limit, the station would get a warning and the engineer would really have to work on it to get it under control. Stations had a certain number of days to do so, before the fines would be enforced. The Federal Communications Commission, regulating interstate and international communications through media of all kinds, did not play.

Rule changes in the 1980s did away with the fixed set of power choices, allowing stations to choose an appropriate power level for their antenna system.

Stations usually range from 1000 watts output all the way up to 50,000 watts. Whereas FM transmitter towers are placed in high places, such as on a hill or mountain, and transmit in a straight line, AM transmits on the ground, penetrating through buildings and other obstacles.

KOA 850, with their focus of sports and news, is an AM Class A radio station that broadcasts with the maximum allowed 50,000 watts. KOA has one of the largest clear channel radio signals in North America, covering much of the western United States. Nicknamed "the Blowtorch of the West," the station was established in 1924.

KDKO increased its power to 5,000 watts in the mid-70s, from its initial 1,000. In the early 90s, shortly after my purchase of the station, we again increased the number of watts, this time to 10,000.

Changing the level of watts was a simple procedure that merely involved flipping a switch, but it became a very complicated process. It had to be approved by the FCC, and engineers needed to be hired in order to take frequent power readings to ensure that the extra wattage did not interfere with other radio station signals. Even in the 70s, the extra wattage cost about a quarter of a million dollars. Twenty years later, that price had risen. Radio is not a low overhead business.

Many people don't realize what it takes to own a radio station. In addition to the red tape for everyone, it is even more compounded when you add being a Black man into the equation.

23 | Notable Names

"A people without the knowledge of their past history, origin, and culture is like a tree without roots."

- Marcus Garvey

I can't begin to go into detail about all the amazing people I have been blessed to know, particularly throughout the years I've spent in Denver.

I will attempt to introduce you to a few of these people who have made a difference both in my own life and that of the community. Many others have touched my being in some way or have been strong voices and activists. This further multitude of individuals perhaps may be part of a sequel.

Born in Chicago, Illinois, Wellington E. Webb grew up in Northeast Denver in the 1940s. He learned the skills and inside knowledge of political involvement from his maternal grandmother Helen M. Gamble, who was active in community affairs in Northeast Denver.

Wellington pursued his post-secondary formal education at the University of Northern Colorado (UNC), then known as Colorado State College. Living in Greeley in the early 60s was fraught with racial challenges. After earning his Bachelor of Arts in sociology, he returned to UNC to receive a master's degree in the same field in 1971.

At one point in his early career, Mr. Webb was turned down twice for teaching positions in Denver Public Schools, so he continued to work as a forklift operator.

I first came to know Wellington personally through shared experience with semi-pro basketball teams in Denver.

Following the assassination of Dr. Martin Luther King, Jr., Denver, like most cities, was in an uproar. I met with a few other people in the community to talk about how we could keep the tension down, and I decided I would start organized basketball opportunities for young people.

We started out at Skyland Park in the Park Hill neighborhood. There's a tennis court now at the site we played ball. I pulled together several businesses to become sponsors. We'd come together and shoot hoops from early in the morning until late in the evening, having competitions.

At that point, the Amateur Athletic Union (AAU) was a popular route for organized boys' basketball. The AAU is an organization that has developed some of the top talents in the country. The national championships held by the AAU offer young athletes of all skill levels a chance to compete for a title, build character, and most of all have fun.

The basketball teams began playing at the Glenarm Recreation Center in the Five Points neighborhood. Randy Redwine was a top basketball player in Colorado, and in the region. He and a couple other star players, including Larry Johnson, approached me to ask if I would consider sponsoring a semi-pro team through the AAU.

"I would love to," was of course my answer.

The games were fundraisers for area schools, particularly parochial schools. The money raised was used to buy milk and food for kids who were unable to have breakfast due to financial issues.

Paul Murray with Murray Brothers Distributors was very involved with parochial schools at that time, the Blessed Sacrament Catholic School in Denver in particular. This school was across the street from Machebeuf High School (now located in the Lowry neighborhood). We broke barriers in these all-white schools by providing some diversity, at least in their gymnasiums.

We would play games all over the city and beyond, from the recreation centers to the state penitentiary. Our KDKO team was responsible for the racial integration of the Salvation Army Red Shield Center near Manual High School. Although laws were in place prohibiting segregation, this Salvation Army was still operating under the underlying subtle segregation policies – an unwritten code saying, "Sorry, we don't have the availability of the space." With our persistence, we were able to play basketball games inside their gymnasium.

When the Martin Luther King, Jr. Recreation Center was built in the Park Hill neighborhood of Denver, it provided an important place for people living in that area to more easily enjoy all the available recreational opportunities; a facility where the surrounding Black community could feel welcome. The KDKO staff, along with the Denver Police Department, planted all the trees that are outside that building.

Before long, I expanded my recruiting to players who had been cut from the Denver Rockets (now the Denver Nuggets). I did my research and sought out the top players in the state. My team would play in tournaments all over the region - New Mexico to Texas to Kansas. The money that they won was how they were paid. No other money was collected for their stipend salaries.

The KDKO All-Stars became very well-known through radio exposure and their winning reputation. If a game was scheduled to start at 2 p.m., you had better get there by 10 a.m. to get a decent seat. People were either fans, or they wanted to see Daddio's All-Stars get beat.

"Getting beat" did not happen very often.

I started out with a vision of playing 100 games, and on the 100th game I gave up the team – after 98 wins. I passed the torch, so to speak, for the KDKO All-Stars to Theirry Smith and Kevin Brown who continued to take the team to many victories.

Wellington Webb had his own semi-pro basketball team, particularly since he had been a star basketball player in college. Beginning with this connection, we became like brothers while we were involved in varied community projects and activism. He and I discovered we had many of the same values and visions, and we both wanted to make a difference politically and otherwise, however we could.

In 1972, Wellington's desire to create genuine and positive change evolved to his election to the Colorado House of Representatives, where he served two terms. We worked hard at KDKO to promote his campaign.

Representative Webb introduced three consecutive bills, beginning in 1975, to make Dr. Martin Luther King, Jr.'s birthday a legal holiday in Colorado. Each of them was met with roadblocks and postponed indefinitely, meaning they were all defeated.

Representative Webb was elected Denver city auditor in 1987, before becoming the first Black mayor in Denver in 1991. In his three terms as mayor, Webb focused primarily on parks and open space, public safety, economic development and children. His development projects included the Denver International Airport, a new sports stadium, expansion of the Denver Arts Museum, and a pride and joy in Five Points – The Blair-Caldwell African American Research Library.

The Wellington E Webb Municipal Office Building was completed in September of 2002 on Colfax Avenue in downtown Denver. The 12-story building was created to be a central location for over 50 city agencies. At this writing, it is currently occupied by the City Auditor's office, the District Attorney's office, Public Works, Planning and Development and the Office of Economic Development, to name only a few of the offices. The 704,000 square foot office building houses over 1800 employees.

♪♪♪

Wellington's wife, Wilma, is the person who ultimately was successful at making Martin Luther King, Jr's birthday an official holiday in Colorado, almost another decade after her husband's efforts. Wilma became a state representative in District 8 in 1980 and continued in that role for 13 years.

She too had put forward three separate bills in 1981,1982, and 1983, before the MLK bill passed in 1984 when she was also a member of the Joint Budget Committee. After the Colorado January holiday became official, Wilma was the creator of the annual Marade in Denver.

When Wilma was a young girl, she heard Martin Luther King, Jr. speak in Denver at New Hope Baptist Church in Denver. Years later, Wilma was an organizer who brought Coretta Scott King to Denver for her first official public speech. They became friends from that time forward.

Mrs. Webb's civic involvement paralleled that of Wellington's. A Denver native, she came from a family of service, her mother a nurse's assistant and her father a federal government employee. Wilma's own political civic involvement began as a community organizer to register voters, assist impoverished families, and encourage equality in education. She holds a graduate degree from the Harvard University John F. Kennedy School of Government.

This dedicated advocate worked closely with her husband in his grassroots mayoral campaign, and during her time as First Lady of the city, focused on anti-drug abuse programs, youth and family issues, and the promotion of the arts in Denver.

In 1998, she became the first woman to serve in the U.S. Department of Labor as the region's chief administrator.

The Webb's have been married since 1969.

♪♪♪

Cleo Parker Robinson founded her namesake dance company in Five Points in 1970. Her ensemble, now based inside the original Shorter Community AME Church building at Washington and 23rd Avenue, has become internationally renowned.

Over the years, Cleo and I had an amazing working relationship, and she became like a sister to me. Cleo was a loyal supporter of KDKO from the beginning. I interviewed her numerous times, both on KDKO and then on my Saturday show on AM 760.

Cleo Parker was brought home from the hospital in 1948 to live in an apartment above the club in the Rossonian Hotel. Her father was a

Black jazz musician/actor and her mother a white classical musician. The mixed couple was more accepted in the context and world of music.

Cleo was personally exposed to and influenced by musicians like Sarah Vaughn, Billie Holiday, Duke Ellington, and Sammy Davis, Jr. – who all performed at the Rossonian. Cleo also grew up seeing artists and activists such as Harry Belafonte and Paul Robeson, who became role models for her.

When Cleo was in Dallas at the age of ten, a segregated hospital refused to admit her for a kidney condition quickly enough to prevent heart failure, and she nearly died. Doctors expected her to be bedridden the rest of her life. She obviously proved them wrong and threw herself into dancing in order to overcome the pain from her physical condition and the emotional challenges of growing up Black.

By age 15 she was teaching university level dance classes at the University of Colorado. She graduated from Colorado Women's College, with a focus on dance, education and psychology.

Cleo Parker Robinson Dance Ensemble has a spirit all its own and remains very much a part of the fabric of the soul of Five Points throughout the ongoing gentrification process of the neighborhood. She strongly believes in the healing power of art and that dance is a universal language.

Cleo married Tom Robinson in 1970 – the prom king when she was prom queen at Regis Jesuit High School in Denver. Tom became the Associate Commissioner for the Colorado High School Activities Association (CHSAA), the first Black administrator in the organization. He passed in 2022. He and Cleo were married for over 50 years.

♪♪♪

Denver native, Hiawatha Davis, graduated from Manual High School, one of the oldest high schools in Denver that opened in 1892 and one of the first schools in Denver to educate African Americans.

During the Vietnam War, Hiawatha was a community activist in the San Francisco area. After he returned to Denver, he was director of Denver Opportunity Neighborhood Programs where he helped organize employment for city youth.

Davis first began his political venture in 1971 with an unsuccessful bid to unseat Councilman Elvin Caldwell in District 8. In 1974, The third time was the charm when he won a Denver City Council seat in 1983.

When he was on the Denver City Council, Hiawatha helped create the Police Review Commission and the Public Nuisance Ordinance. I appreciated how he always tried to speak for the so-called voiceless in the community, not only chipping away at racism, but sexism and poverty as well.

He worked to help people find affordable housing, advocated for senior services, promoted historic preservation, and reached out to those who had been imprisoned. This tireless Denver activist was a leader in the fight to stop gang violence in Denver. He and I had a similar passion for using our voice to help others, and agreed if there was no struggle, there was no progress.

Davis served five terms on Denver City Council. In 1999, after winning re-election, he quit the city council to become the Executive Director of the Agency for Human Rights and Community Relations under Mayor Wellington E. Webb.

Sadly, in 2000, Hiawatha lost a battle to prostate cancer at the age of only 56. At his funeral service, I'll never forget how Pastor Acen Phillips described Davis.

"There are not too many people who can shake the tree and also catch the apples. We've all had applesauce and some apple pie because of Hiawatha Davis."

In 2001, Denver Parks and Recreation reopened Skyland Recreation Center in Park Hill as the Hiawatha Davis, Jr. Recreational Center, after a $4.5 million expansion and remodel project.

♪♪♪

Les Franklin, a Colorado Springs native, worked throughout high school as the night manager at a nightclub/restaurant owned by his aunt. His single mother, Selena Bragg, worked there as well.

Les received an athletic scholarship to the University of Northern Colorado and earned a business degree. From there, Les enlisted for four years in the United States Air Force, becoming a lieutenant. After returning home to Colorado, Les got a job at IBM. He continued to receive job promotions that gave him the opportunity to be an "executive on loan;" as the chair of the Los Angeles office of the United Negro College Fund. I remember him telling me stories about hob-knobbing with greats like Sammy Davis, Jr, Redd Foxx, and Elizabeth Taylor. He came back to Colorado to serve as director of the job training office under Governor Roy Romer.

Tragically, in 1990, the Franklin's 16-year-old son, Shaka, took his own life with a self-inflicted gunshot wound. Shaka had lost hope with his mother's failing health, and a season ending football injury. They also suspect a head injury from a bicycle accident a few years before may have also contributed.

Les resigned from his job and created the Shaka Franklin Foundation for Youth (SFF) to raise awareness and provide education and support for the complex issue of suicide. SFF has participated in numerous television interviews over the years, including the Today Show, Montel Williams and the Donahue Show. Les and his second wife, Marianne, have tirelessly and humbly devoted everything they have to the Foundation. Marianne serves as the president and executive director of SFF.

The Shaka Foundation provided at-risk young people with activities such as ice hockey and figure skating, as well as a recording studio and a computer lab to help instill self-confidence and give other alternatives. The Foundation currently also provides scholarships to promote advancement in mental health careers; helps secure mental health services for those impacted by suicide and offers opportunities for community engagement.

A decade after their devastating loss, the unthinkable happened to the family a second time when son Jamon, a graduate of Morehouse College, lost his life to carbon monoxide poisoning in the garage at the age of 31.

Sometimes, no matter how hard we try, it can be impossible to prevent things that befall us. There's a statistic out there that the risk of suicide is thought to be up to 12 times higher for people whose immediate family members have taken their own lives.

The Shaka Foundation marked the 29th anniversary of the annual Love Our Children benefit luncheon in 2019. The uplifting and inspiring event always included the presentation of a Youth Legacy Award and raised hundreds of thousands of dollars to support the valiant efforts of this incredible foundation.

Les was a true friend and brother, but he and I are no longer in regular contact. Life's relationships ebb and flow.

♪♪♪

An Alabama native and youngest of nine siblings, Moses Brewer was a star basketball athlete at the University of Denver (DU) in the late 1960s, which shouldn't surprise anyone with his 6'4" stature.

Moses graduated from DU with a bachelor's in physical education and recreation, then returned to complete his master's in speech communications and human relations. He went on to work for DU as an associate dean of student affairs and an assistant men's basketball coach. Moses has remained very connected to his alma mater and created an endowment at DU in his name about four years ago to support men's basketball.

Most people in the Denver community know Moses as the Manager of Community Commerce and Partnerships/Multicultural Relations Director at MillerCoors, originally Coors Brewing Company. He retired in 2014 after holding that position for 31 years.

Thanks to the efforts of Moses Brewer, Coors did a lot for the African American community. Moses was involved with many local and national African American organizations implementing marketing initiatives and sponsoring various events and scholarships. In 2013, the Commerce and Community Partnerships Department at Coors orchestrated the donation of $1.3 million to the Thurgood Marshall College Fund, which provides scholarships to 47 HBCUs – due to the efforts of this dedicated community leader.

Moses came into my life early on, when I first came to Denver. He was a supporter of KDKO from the beginning and was always a remarkable brother to me. Moses was always a great connective link between Coors and the Black community.

He would always say the three most important things you can say are I'm sorry, thank you, and I love you.

As a side note, I was also a fan of William Coors, a brewery executive of Coors Brewing Company and a grandson of the company's founder, Adolph Coors. Bill agreed to advertise on KDKO after I had struggled for years with the advertising agency in the brewing company.

It just goes to show, it is always good to go straight to the top!

♪♪♪

One of the various shows Paul Mack and I promoted with Donny Hathaway was at a college campus in Oakland, California. When I arrived at the concert hall, the performance had started. As I entered the box office, I saw this man counting money from the ticket sales. I wondered who the Hell was this guy handling our profits.

He introduced himself as Lu Vason.

I learned that Lu was a friend of Paul's and an active promoter in the Bay area, with many groups including The Pointer Sisters, The Whispers, and others. We connected quickly through our shared promotion context.

Back in Denver, Gene DeWitt approached me about becoming his promotion person. Gene was bringing in many entertainers, such as Gladys Knight, Smokey Robinson, The Temptations, The Pointer Sisters, Nancy Wilson, The Whispers, and Lou Rawls to The Warehouse, a popular dinner club and entertainment spot that Gene owned in Glendale at the corner of Leetsdale and Alameda.

"I'm doing my own thing and have the radio station," I told him. "I just don't have the time, but I can hook you up with someone in California who has been talking about coming to Colorado."

Lu moved his family to Denver in 1977. We became increasingly closer friends and supported one another in our respective endeavors. He and I shared a fascination with history. Lu was always intrigued with rodeo, and after attending the Cheyenne Frontier Days, he was perplexed by the lack of Black competitors.

He immediately began his quest to further explore this topic and discovered the information he was looking for at the Black American West Museum in Five Points. Lu learned that an estimated quarter of the West's cowboys were Black, many headed to the open range after freedom from enslavement in the South. In 1984, Lu founded the Bill Pickett Invitational Rodeo, named after a renowned Black cowboy. This famous Black rodeo continues to tour across the United States each year.

Lu continued to bring many amazing concerts and Jazz Festivals to Denver until his passing in 2015. I re-broadcast his funeral on my Saturday afternoon program on AM 760.

Lu was always the glue that kept his friends connected. He would bring Moses Brewer, Les Franklin, Jim Wheeler, Nelson Ball, himself and me together for a Taurus party each spring to observe our birthdays.

We continue to celebrate you, Lu.

♪♪♪

Aurora's first African American police chief, Nick Metz, retired in 2019, after 36 years of working in law enforcement. During his five years as the Aurora police chief, Metz weathered many storms and some high-profile controversies. I always admired his willingness to develop relationships with people, some who didn't always agree with him. Even with disagreement, there was always respect.

Back in college, he was thinking about studying mortuary science to follow in family footsteps. But then, he ended up tagging along with an officer doing a week-long ride along for a college class. That experience changed his life's trajectory.

Officer Metz began his career with the Seattle Police department when he was 20 and grew in the department to become assistant police chief. He was hired as the Aurora chief due to his experience in a diverse city.

During his time in Aurora, Metz or a representative reportedly attended nearly every NAACP meeting and many other community meetings as well.

When Denver Police Chief Robert White left, I gave Chief Metz regular time on my Saturday program on AM 760.

Unlike many officers, Chief Metz left on his own choice and merit, and he did not retire from helping people or community. He wanted to continue to help other officers manage the stress and trauma that goes along with the work. At the time of his retirement, it was his plan to work with his wife in her counseling practice for first responders.

♪♪♪

Reverend Reginald Holmes, a native of Stuart, Florida, is co-pastor at New Covenant Christian Church / Alpha Omega Ministries in Denver. He is past president of the Greater Metro Denver Ministerial Alliance and a longtime civil rights advocate in Denver.

New Covenant was founded as a "mission church" in 1950. Park Hill was the initial designation of its mission work and location, so the church was originally named Park Hill Christian Church. Since the neighborhood at that time was white, it was a white congregation. During the 1960s, those demographics switched up and it became a predominantly African American church.

Reverend Holmes became their pastor in 1988. By that time, the church had moved out of Park Hill, and its name was changed to New Covenant Christian Church in 1997.

In 2014, Holmes joined New Covenant with Pastor Terrence "Big T" Hughes' Alpha Omega Ministries. Theirs is an ever-adapting ministry, which focuses on true Christian service – regularly feeding and helping the homeless population in the neighborhood - and community activism.

I have always been a large proponent of helping further the Black churches of Denver by advertising and promoting their individual ministries and services. I've developed friendships and stayed connected with many of the pastors.

Reginald Holmes is closer to me than most. Not only because of his strong and sincere activism in social justice issues, but especially after a poignant experience that will always stay with me. When Pastor Holmes' father passed in 1995, he went home to give the Eulogy at the funeral service. Reginald taped his Eulogy and we broadcast it on KDKO. It was one of the most touching things I have ever heard. His Tribute to his dad spoke so highly of Pastor Holmes' character. Particularly after that, we became very close, like brothers, and we talk every day. We're fishing buddies, who always give each other the daily fishing report.

We would broadcast his church services on the radio, and he has told me that he feels like he built his church through KDKO, and that most of his ministry was formed as a result of his airtime.

When we ran into some financial difficulties with the station, Pastor Holmes was right there with his church. They gave to the effort and members of his congregation came down to the station and submitted the offering on air.

His giving spirit is something that I greatly admire. One of his mottos is "Life will get no better for me until I help make it better for someone else."

He and I have an uncanny ability to find meaning in the adversity that seems to befall us on our fishing trips. On one trip, we were on our way home driving near La Junta on a desolate highway when we got a flat tire on Holmes' car. He had taken the jack out of his car, and I had recently had back surgery. I assured him that someone would stop to help, and all would be fine.

Sure enough, the good Lord came through for us and a cattle truck pulled over to assist us. The driver had all the necessary tools, and in the meantime another trucker stopped to help as well. We got back on our highway, both tired and more than ready to get home again after our unexpected delay. Not ten miles down the road, we came across an older couple needing roadside assistance. We looked at each other and knew, without a doubt, that we could do nothing else except stop to help them out.

I had a business card from a state trooper who had stayed with us when Pat and I had car trouble several months prior. I called him and he sent another officer to come and pick up this couple.

It turns out, the pair had driven all the way from Phoenix on their way to Chicago. The state patrol put the couple up in a hotel for a few days while they had their engine replaced in their car.

There is importance in always "paying it forward."

Recently, Pastor Holmes shared details of another bout of car trouble when he was with his son, and how it had all turned out well.

He told me, "Anytime I have problems now, you come into my mind with your positiveness, and I know it will get taken care of."

♪♪♪

I met Peggy Wortham after I purchased KDKO. Her husband at the time, J. Wallace Wortham, Jr. (Wally) and I were good friends. She has always been a strong community activist and when Wellington Webb put in his 1991 Denver mayoral bid, Peggy hit the ground running, joining his infamous "Sneaker Campaign," where he walked a large portion of the city introducing himself door to door.

Peggy became a "right hand person" for Webb and gave him so much support. When he won his second term, I was very happy Wellington made Peggy his official press assistant. He certainly never regretted that decision, for both his second and third term. Among so many different accomplishments, Peggy assisted the mayor with bringing he and Wilma's vision of the Blair-Caldwell African American Research Library and the Denver City Park Dr. Martin Luther King, Jr, statue into reality. Webb named Wally the city attorney in 2000.

I soon realized Peggy's astute attention to detail, and she became a primary person of connection for me. Anything one needs to know about anyone in the city, no matter what color, Peggy is the person to call. If she doesn't have an immediate answer, give her a few minutes or at most a day, and she will be sure to get back with the information.

Peggy helped me out a great deal with Fair Share Jobs. She would keep me informed on job openings for employment opportunities and helped with promotional activities as well. Peggy and her daughters, Jill and Michele, often helped in the Fair Share office in Aurora.

She worked as the office manager and membership coordinator for the Colorado Black Chamber of Commerce and has been involved with numerous other sectors including the office of former Governor Dick Lamm, the Urban League of Metropolitan Denver, and the United Negro College Fund. Although retired, Peggy continues to work with the Bill Pickett Invitational Rodeo and is an associate member of the Buffalo Soldiers Motorcycle Club Mile High Chapter.

Peggy has received numerous awards including a Juanita Gray Community Service Award, a Colorado Black Women for Political Action Award, and a Colorado Black Roundtable "Black Women Who Get It Done in the Community" Award. I'm glad that others also recognize her outstanding contributions to Denver.

Peggy is a great friend, and she and I continue to talk often.

♪♪♪

Rosalind "Bee" Harris grew up in Grand Rapids, Michigan. She pursued her education in fashion merchandising, graphic design, mass communications and fine arts. Bee co-founded a graphic design freelance business, Salt and Pepper Art Studios, in Omaha, Nebraska which thrived for many years.

Seven years after moving to Denver, Bee founded the *Denver*

Urban Spectrum newspaper in 1987 and has been spreading the news about people of color in her impressive monthly publication ever since. In 2000, Bee started the Urban Spectrum Youth Foundation, a mentoring program that trained youth from 11 to 17 in the field of journalism – teaching skills and techniques in writing, reporting, photography, layout, sales, marketing and business management during a seven-week summer journalism camp

Over the years, Bee has always coordinated and participated in a number of community outreach projects. When Hurricane Katrina struck New Orleans in 2005, she and her team created an invaluable resource and entertainment fair in Denver providing needed networking and support to displaced survivors. This is just one example of the many important events Bee provides to the community.

I give Bee so much credit for where she is today, the publisher and art director of the minority woman-owned family-operated business for 35 years and counting. She has had many ups and downs; she is truly a fighter, a good person, and a dear friend. We've supported each other in all our respective business ventures.

♪♪♪

East High graduate Vikki Buckley worked at Pat's Record Parlor as one of her first jobs. In 1994, Ms. Buckley was elected the 32nd Secretary of State in Colorado and the nation's highest ranking Black female Republican in a statewide office at the time. As Secretary of State, Vikki stressed improving customer service in businesses, and impressively returned $9 million to the state treasury from office fees.

She pursued her dream of success through hard work and self-sufficiency, overcoming many challenges through her determination. In

1998, Secretary of State Buckley was elected to a second term. Sadly, only seven months into her renewed appointment, she passed away from undiagnosed sarcoidosis at the age of 49.

She had a radio program on KDKO, and we broadcast her funeral service. I was close to Vikki and her family. Her sister, Pat Duncan, a notable photographer and author in Denver, has steadfastly ensured that Vikki's legacy remains alive.

♪♪♪

Another important political voice was Joe Rogers, becoming the second African American and the youngest lieutenant governor in Colorado history when he won by a wide margin with running mate Bill Owens in 1998. Joe was a very caring person, well-known for helping those in need with free legal services. He was my attorney and like a son to me; so intelligent, genuine and a true groundbreaker. He also left this realm way too soon in 2013 at only 49 years old.

♪♪♪

I cannot complete this book without writing more about Ray Hambric, my broker, my close friend, my brother. When I was beginning my radio station purchase journey, I heard about this accountant guy who had become a radio broker and he had a reputation of helping the underdog.

The day I met Ray, I walked into his office and said, "I'm Dr. Daddio. I want to buy a radio station, and somebody told me you might be able to help me."

"You came to the right place. That's what I do," was Ray's reply.

From there began a voyage of hard work and determination. We put together a business plan and we were on our way. There were many ups and downs through our initial first attempts at our purchase of KDKO. Ray stuck with me through it all. He was my guy, my right hand.

As Ray would say, "Sometimes it felt like we were fighting with only one arm."

He has always been dedicated and committed to any mission he set his sights on. We immediately clicked in our personalities, an appreciation of nature, and a love of biscuits and gravy. The bottom line is we just liked each other. With the amount of time we were spending together putting all the business pieces in place, we could not help but learn a great deal about one another's interests and temperaments. We're two boys from the south; he was born on a farm in Alabama.

When the cotton mills were closing, Ray's father loaded the family in a pickup truck and headed to Colorado. His dad got a job at a steel mill in Pueblo, Colorado Fuel and Iron Company (CF&I).

With no interest in the field that he was aware of, Ray took an accounting class and found he was good with numbers. After attending Pueblo Junior College (now Colorado State University Pueblo), he continued at the University of Colorado in Boulder to earn his accounting degree and went to work as a public accountant at a large firm. He soon learned that corporate America was not for him, so he became an entrepreneur. He evolved into the field of radio and radio brokering after putting together a deal for a radio station in Omaha, Nebraska - the management failed, and he went there to run the station.

He is my accountant in all of my business endeavors and our friendship continues to grow. Ray has told me that helping to bring Black ownership to Denver has been his greatest accomplishment to date. He is like a blood brother to me, and we would put our lives on the line for each other.

I visit him whenever I get a chance on his beautiful ranch in Rye, Colorado. He drove two and a half hours to be at Pat's memorial service. Ray thought it was so amazing; he said he wants a service just like hers when his time comes. My daughter told him she would work on it for him to make sure it happens.

In the meantime, we are on an ongoing quest for the best biscuits and gravy in the state. Ray thinks they might be in Walsenburg, Colorado, so we will be going there soon.

♪♪♪

It was hard to decide what part of this book to talk about Jeff Fard, for years now known as brother jeff in the community. He has been an ongoing part of my life for the last five decades as a young mentee, a valuable part of KDKO, a community activist, and I've always considered him to be one of my own sons.

He grew up in Northeast Denver as a common fixture at my house since he is around the same age as my oldest son, Ricky. I disciplined him as if he were my own son and watched him grow and learn.

As a young man, I took him under my wing at the station with his strong interest in radio and music. He had gotten deeply involved in the Denver HIP-HOP scene and was part of one of the most popular groups in Denver, Legend of Doom.

Brother jeff worked as an on-air personality at KDKO as "Mr. Magic." He became my assistant program director under Terry Hutt, and later directed the internship program at the station. This internship program that continued through the years of KDKO produced many well-known radio personalities, among them Tony V, Jason McBride, and Jeffrey "Kingdom" McWhorter. Jeff became a valuable part of the station, and of all that has evolved since.

His commitment to music became a commitment to community and I watched him grow into a grassroots organizer. Brother jeff has followed in my footsteps in giving a voice to the community, particularly to those who are often not heard. His tagline embodies his work, and who he is: "SAY IT LOUD."

In 1994, he founded brother jeff's Cultural Center on Welton Street, which continues to be an integral part of Five Points, even when so many businesses and residents have succumbed to the often-insurmountable challenges and inevitable changes of gentrification.

In its early days, the Cultural Center began holding events that were counter to gang culture, while also addressing systemic reasons for their resulting destructive behavior. Now home to many varied events, from community meetings to Jazz, HIP-HOP, and spoken word poetry, it continues to be a welcoming space committed to fostering strength and unity, providing a place where everyone is valued, appreciated and respected for who they are.

In 2000, brother jeff began organizing state-wide and nationally to help reduce the disproportional rate of HIV and AIDS in the Black community. He served as an advisor to the Centers of Disease Control and Prevention, the Colorado Department of Public Health and Environment, as well as other organizations dedicated to education and prevention of HIV.

Over the years, his focus has expanded to gun violence reduction, police brutality issues, mental health interventions, and community mentor development. He speaks locally and nationally to youth, business and non-profit organizations, and other professionals about issues of cultural identity and history, diversity, self-empowerment, community building, and economic development. Brother jeff is the publisher of the monthly community newspaper, *5 STAR NEWS*, formerly *5 POINTS NEWS*.

Throughout brother jeff's years as a community activist and integral part of Denver, I have always been very impressed with his vision and his goals, and how he carries himself as a leader. He has learned how to deal with and work within the system in such a positive way, with an art of diplomacy and the ability to work with all different types of people. I have watched him plan and carry out events, and they seem to come off like magic.

Brother jeff hosts Black Dollar Saturday every week at the Cultural Center, providing local entrepreneurs an opportunity to sell their goods and continuing the legacy of Black businesses on Welton Street

I am so very proud of the leader, and the man, he is today.

To the many people I have not yet mentioned, you all know who you are, and I am eternally grateful to each and every one of you.

24 | Five Points

"Unity is strength, division is weakness."

- Swahili Proverb

Five Points was a magical place when Patsy and I arrived in Denver. Because Blacks were restricted in where they were allowed to live, Five Points became a Black neighborhood, with Black-owned businesses, churches and social civic organizations. Even though this was already beginning to shift when we moved here from Houston, the community was still booming. We were drawn to Five Points as it was a community of individuals who wanted to protect and preserve the legacy that had been established.

The name of Five Points came into existence in 1881 because the signs on the front of the streetcars weren't large enough to hold all the street names that converged into one point. This five-way intersection includes 27th Street, Washington Street, East 26th Avenue, and Welton Street.

By the early 1890s more African Americans lived in Five Points than any other part of the city due to segregation and an increase in railroad and industrial jobs in the area. In addition, more Blacks were leaving the South to escape the repressive Jim Crow Laws and moving farther west. By the late 1920s, Five Points had become an almost all Black neighborhood.

However, all was not always better in the West. In the 1920s, Ku Klux Klan activity was at an all-time high in Denver. Colorado was second only to Indiana with 50,000 declared members. KKK participants were elected to government roles, including Governor Clarence Morley, state legislators, Denver's mayor Ben Stapleton, Supreme Court judges, and Denver Chief of Police William Candlish. Discriminatory neighborhood covenants were enforced, banning whites from selling homes or property to non-whites outside of Five Points.

Despite these adversities, Historic Five Points was a nationally recognized vibrant Black cultural center beginning in the early 20th century, widely known as the "Harlem of the West." The community thrived through the mid-century with a rich mix of local business and commerce along Welton. At one point, the Welton Street business district was the largest Black business community in the West, providing jobs, education and skills to its residents.

One common theme in the history of Five Points has always been the music – particularly jazz. The music was the rhythm of the neighborhood. Music brings people together like glue. It molds, it blends, and it doesn't discriminate. Democracy is experienced with jazz, because that's what jazz is. It gives everyone a chance at expression within a collective framework.

Five Points has always been a very welcoming community in connection to its music. This is a community that helped nurture and bring this trait forward across all barriers, including race and class.

KDEN was Denver's first radio station to play jazz over the airwaves. The station was started in 1957 by Ed Koepke and Gene Amole as a mostly classical station, but at 5 p.m. on weekdays, *The*

Art of Jazz, hosted by Gene, could be found on AM 1340. In 1973, KDEN changed its format to all news.

There were so many memorable people and establishments in Five Points. The Rossonian Hotel, a central entertainment venue in the heart of Five Points, was originally known as The Baxter Hotel until 1929. Its first-floor lounge gained the reputation as the best jazz club between the Midwest and the West Coast.

Back in the day, The Rossonian hosted Nat King Cole, Count Basie, Lionel Hampton, Billie Holiday, Ella Fitzgerald, and Duke Ellington, along with other musical legends. Black entertainers stayed at the hotel when they came to perform at other locations in Denver as often the downtown white hotels would turn them away. Five Points became a hub for these artists and an after-hours spot for impromptu performances.

When I came to Denver, The Rossonian was an exclusive entertainment club, featuring primarily jazz. By the 1950s, the word was out about this vibrant destination spot and its reputation had spread throughout Colorado and beyond. It then became more the "white side" of entertainment because the tickets outpriced most of the community and neighborhood residents. Frank Sinatra, Nancy Wilson, and Sammy Davis, Jr. were some of the main performers. Sadly, the crown jewel of Five Points closed within the next decade from when I arrived.

Across the street, The Casino Cabaret, opened by world renowned violinist and orchestra leader George Morrison in the 1920s, was more the "Black side" of entertainment after The Rossonian became more exclusive. B.B. King, James Brown, Bobby Bland, and other blues' artists were feature attractions.

The Protective Order of Dining Car Waiters, Local #465 was the original name when it was established in 1937 – a place where one had to climb 19 steep steps to enter. It transitioned into the Porter's and Waiter's Club, and finally M&M's, a popular bar until around 2015. And who could ever forget Kapre Chicken, the Arcade, or the 715 Club?

Rice's Tap Room had already closed when I moved here. It had been an established fixture in Five Points for many years. Otha Rice moved to Five Points from Texas and opened this central and popular spot. There had been a jazz and blues club, a bar, and a restaurant on the first floor. The Simmons Hotel was on the second floor.

Woodsman Insurance was the only Black insurance company that I had ever known or had any experience with throughout my entire life. The insurance company was known nationally, and at one point they employed more Blacks than any other business in Denver. Tom Yates was the owner at the time I moved to Denver.

Fire Station No. 3, originally located at 2563 Glenarm Place and coined "Pride of the Points," was the only fire station where Blacks could work. It opened in 1888 as Steamer Company 3 and became part of the Denver Fire Department after 1892. The station moved catty-corner to 2500 Washington St. in 1931 and was segregated until 1951. Charles Cousins, Jr. worked there as a firefighter.

The Roxy was the theatre, and the first African American movie house in Denver. It opened in 1934 during the heart of The Great Depression, and the admission price to see a movie was five cents. Charles Cousins, Jr. owned the Roxy when we moved to Denver, and he converted it to a night club.

Charles "Brother" Cousins, Jr. and McKinley Harris were two

of the greatest and most prominent leaders in Five Points when I arrived. Charles owned most of the property in the neighborhood and McKinley controlled the real estate.

Charles Cousins, Sr. was born in Virginia in the late 1800s. Moving to Denver in 1909 with his wife and children, he worked as a Pullman porter for the Union Pacific and Santa Fe railroads for 33 years. In his spare time, Mr. Cousins enjoyed watching the construction of major buildings in Denver. In 1915, he built his first duplex at 26th Avenue and High Street. He saved his earnings, and the restrictive covenants motivated him to acquire more and more property in Five Points to provide affordable housing in the neighborhood. The senior Cousins had passed by the time I came to town, so I only heard these amazing stories from his family.

Charles Cousins, Jr. would go to all the city meetings, which is why he was able to successfully own so much property to add to what his father left him and his brother. Charles graduated from Manual High School and was a licensed building contractor for many decades. He followed in his father's footsteps by providing housing and financial support for people who wanted to further themselves in business or education, as well as employing several people in the community. Mr. Cousins was also a boxing commissioner who had relationships with Heavyweight Champions Joe Lewis and Muhammad Ali.

McKinley Harris started out working with Sonny Lawson in real estate. Lawson, a Denver native, was also known for his political activism. He opened Radio Pharmacy in Five Points and ran it for more than 50 years. He was the district executive for the Democratic Party in East Denver for nearly a quarter of a century. In 1972, a park on Welton Street was named Sonny Lawson Park, the first in Denver to be named after an African American.

In 1955, Mr. Harris started Public Realty Company on Welton Street. The business offered loans, employment services, and real estate assistance. Restrictive covenants, racism and segregation were very real roadblocks to African Americans wanting to buy a home or property, so this was one of the most imperative businesses to have available in the Black community. Mr. Harris passed the neighborhood institution on to his sons, Patrick and Verne, and Public Realty Company continues to thrive, now located on Bruce Randolph Avenue.

Norman Harris, Sr. (no relation to McKinley Harris) was very powerful as well. Mr. Harris co-owned the Wise-Harris Arms apartments on Welton, which his family kept until 2016. He was also an influential leader in Five Points and was another supportive mentor to me when I came to Denver. An Air Force veteran, one of his hallmark traits, well into his 90s, was every day sweeping the sidewalk in front of his building, cleaning every crevice. He was a meticulous and detail-oriented person, having worked as a computer programmer in the 1960s. He also owned two liquor stores, where he let people run tabs that he'd tally on brown paper bags. Every morning, as long as he was able, he would go for a mile and a half walk around the Five Points neighborhood.

Norman, Sr. continued operating his residential units until he was 98 years old. I went to his 99th birthday party in 2017. It was the same year he passed.

Leroy Smith, Denver's first official Black disc jockey, was a go-getter and community activist I came to know when I settled in Denver.

The Oklahoma native moved to Denver in 1936, and by 1945 he was the youngest 33rd degree Mason in Colorado. From 1948 to 1960, he had a 30-minute midnight show, Rockin' with Leroy, on a station called KFEL. He paid for his airtime and brought his own records. He opened doors for Black entertainers to come to Denver.

This leader of entertainment had the only record store that I can remember being here at that time; Rhythm Records and Sports Shop sold both records and sporting goods, becoming the third largest sporting goods business in America at one time. Another record store opened in Five Points a few years later, Selman Records.

In the 1960s, Mr. Smith converted an apartment/office building and started the Colorado Negro Voter's Club. A friend and promoter of Muhammad Ali, he was the first African American to join the Denver Chamber of Commerce, and also became the deputy game warden in Colorado.

Benny Hooper was one of the greatest of the greats. He had the title of the "Mayor of Five Points," and he was well known for his charitable service. He owned the Ex-Servicemen's Club on Welton Street. Due to the discrimination that Black soldiers returning from World War I were experiencing at restaurants, clubs and hotels, Mr. Hooper opened his own club with a ballroom, pool hall, recreation center, and hotel.

There were several plumbing businesses in the neighborhood, Moore Plumbing, Roundtree Plumbing, and Estes Plumbing. Other notable people included Bishop Hunter with the electric company, Alex Duncan with Duncan's Men's Store, and Crayton Jones with C&B Cleaners. Among the last of the legacy businesses, after 58 years, Jones sold his property and left Welton Street in 2016.

There were of course women who were groundbreakers and incredible leaders in Five Points as well. Dr. Justina Ford began her physician practice as Denver's only Black woman medical doctor. She worked out of her home and office at 23rd and Arapahoe from 1902 to1952. Her house is now the site of the Black American West Museum & Heritage Center.

Mrs. Wheeler, of Mrs. Wheelers Barber Shop, was one of the most established barbers in the city when I got here. She later moved to the Dahlia Square in Park Hill and operated there.

Charlene's House of Beauty was a fixture on Welton Street for over 60 years. Charlene Jordan moved from the South to pursue her dream of opening a beauty salon, offering cosmetics, skin care and hair services.

Franklin Stiger Afro Styling Barber Shop and Five Points Beauty & Barber are two legacy businesses that continue to operate on Welton Street.

Many of these great legends of Five Points had a significant impact on me. After I arrived in Denver, it was important to me to learn as much as I could from their experience and wisdom. I spent as much time as I was able, listening to their stories and all they were willing to share. That's how I learned the city. When I came here, I wanted to know everything there was to know. Just as at the radio station when I was learning the business, I had a notebook where I wrote down everything all these individuals could tell me, the community history, their own accomplishments, their struggles and their triumphs.

I know that shadowing these great figures is part of what made me who I am today. I tell young people all the time: if there is something you want to do and do well, go to the individuals who can help you and get you to that point. I spent hours and hours doing just that. They became my mentors.

I also gained a number of mentors from the Colorado Q's, a group comprised of the Denver Black elite, many of whom were Manual and East High graduates. This insightful collective included people such as Otha Rice, Charles Cousins, Jr., George Morrison, Jr., Marjorie Morrison, Oscar Lynch, Geneva Whitney, Marie L. Greenwood, Jessie Morrison, Frances M. Currin, Ralph McVey, among many others. They would hold an annual conference at The Holiday Inn in Cherry Creek, taking up the entire hotel. This is where I also received so much valuable information about the city, its history and its people. There was overlap with my discovered Five Points wisdom, as some of my incredible neighborhood mentors were a part of the Colorado Q's as well.

Arkansas native "Daddy Bruce" Randolph was one of my closest and most valuable mentors. He was like a dad to me.

Daddy Bruce donated thousands of dollars, as well as hours, to provide clothing and meals to the homeless. He became most well-known in Denver and beyond for his annual Thanksgiving dinners, providing holiday meals to more than 20,000 people each year. Before coming to Colorado, he ran multiple restaurants, a hotel, and a taxi-cab business in Pampa, Texas.

I first met Daddy Bruce in his son's, Bruce, Jr.'s, barbershop where I had my hair cut for more than 20 years. Before Bruce, Sr. opened his own restaurant in Denver, he set up tables in the barbershop and began barbequing for the patrons. Daddy Bruce had taken a job as a janitor just so he could buy a large smoker.

Before long, large organizations were asking him to cater their events; the Denver Broncos among those seeking his service. Eventually, the team would take him to games in other states to cook for the players and staff

I was drawn to Daddy Bruce's dedication and hard work, and so once again I grabbed my trusty notebook and spent as much time with him as I could. The more I got to know him, the more I admired him. Daddy Bruce was very committed to helping people. He worked so hard and invested all his income back into those who were in need. He was beyond an entrepreneur; he was a true philanthropist.

Daddy Bruce is a great example of level of education not equating to the amount of knowledge to be had. With his third-grade education, this man imparted more lessons on what really matters in life than most anyone I have been around.

When the city of Denver tried to shut his restaurant down, I did a remote broadcast with KDKO and raised the money needed to help him. I was involved in everything this incredible humanitarian did, including memorable live remotes at his Thanksgiving dinner giveaways. And he always gave me the same loyal support. He was an amazing teacher in his selfless giving and support of his community.

When he passed at the age of 94, Daddy Bruce's son gave me his father's boat.

In his memory, I would quote his favorite saying on KDKO, and add to it. "God loves you, Daddy Bruce loves you...and I love you too."

It was a gift for me to spend so much time in the presence of the unique and varied individuals that made up the fabric and the rich tapestry of Five Points. They are people who were born in Five Points, and people who found their home in Five Points. They are people who lived and worked in the community with a passion for preserving its rich history.

It was both a blessing and a curse that Blacks were once restricted in where they were allowed to live. Although controlling and limiting, the restrictiveness also created a community, with a bond and determination that made the Five Points neighborhood thrive. There wasn't a choice other than to rely on one another. Dreams were allowed and realized.

♪♪♪

When Blacks were able to move beyond Five Points across Colorado Boulevard and into the Denver Park Hill neighborhood, the previously all-white Dahlia Square began to fill with Black-owned businesses. This new development boomed with so many different establishments; among them a beauty shop, a barber shop, a dry cleaner, liquor stores, a bowling alley, a carpet store, a real estate office, a department store, an appliance center, an auto parts store, Cosmo Harris' *Denver Weekly News* newspaper, and Pat's Record Parlor.

My wife and I both saw the creative opportunity in her record store. The distributors were at our fingertips, and through our KDKO connections, Pat and I could work as a team to have the music available for hungry record connoisseurs. We had the inside tracks on the number one records. James Brown was a great influence at that time. Every record that he produced for himself or his stars, we were able to get hundreds of copies.

The majority of the businesses in the Dahlia Square were Black-owned at that time. Though white-owned, the King Soopers in the Dahlia was Black-managed. In my opinion, the white system had to create a change to this success and prosperity in a Black community. There were people watching what was happening. Articles began to appear in the newspapers claiming a high level of theft in the grocery store and accusing the Black store managers of allowing this stealing to happen.

Similar non-Black businesses and shops began to appear in the area in an attempt to drive other establishments out. As the Black worker was getting paid, the dollars were being spent at the most convenient businesses. Over the years, white owned operations continued being built, and buying out what was existing, forcing the Black-owned community in the neighborhood out of business.

♪♪♪

"When morality comes up against profit, it is seldom that profit loses."

- Shirley Chisholm

Gentrification, sometimes referred to as urban gentrification, is defined by the American Heritage Dictionary as *the restoration and upgrading of deteriorated urban property by middle-class or affluent people, often resulting in the displacement of people with lower income.*

The process of gentrification has been happening for years all over our country, and the world.

The Five Points community had already begun to change when I arrived in 1966. Integration, middle-class flight of African Americans seeking new housing after discriminatory housing became illegal, and the declining economy were all contributing factors to the shifts in the neighborhood through the next several decades.

During the 1980s, drug prevalence, gang violence, and so-called "blight" was unfortunately becoming more prominent. Many properties were abandoned, the local economy became somewhat irrelevant, and the neighborhood saw an extreme shift from its heyday just a few decades earlier.

The 1980s were ripe with deflated housing and property values, and the process of gentrification began in earnest. Wealthier residents craving the appeal of an urban atmosphere started to move in from the suburbs. This influx inevitably resulted in the spark of an urban renewal process with affluent newcomers, leading to an increase in property value, rent, and taxes coupled with conflict, displacement of long-time residents, and marginalization.

It was still important for me to move KDKO into the neighborhood and community that had so much rich history and meaning to me. This is where I felt at home, surrounded by legacy.

Five Points is now a different neighborhood. Emerging from The Great Recession of 2007-2009, in the heart of gentrification, million-dollar lofts and multi-million-dollar developments grew right across the street from places such as the St. Francis Center, Stout Street Health Center, Denver Rescue Mission, Samaritan House, and other non-profit organizations, that serve a vast homeless population.

The inevitable changes have sadly brought high rises all along the Welton Street corridor. The dissenting voices trying to create a place at the table for everyone could not stop this process of bringing monetary wealth and the colonizers into the Points. Five Points has moved in the direction of the "Haves," at the expense of the "Have Nots. And that divide continues to widen.

If there is good news among this shift, it is that the legacy of Five Points is being sustained through Black ownership of new businesses on Welton Street, the renewal of the annual Juneteenth celebration by Norman Harris III, the ongoing efforts of brother jeff's Cultural Center, the continuation of jazz with festivals and ongoing music, and the determination of those who will never forget.

A branch of the Denver Public Library, the Blair-Caldwell African American Research Library opened in 2003 in the heart of Five Points on Welton Street. A research library with collections focusing on the history of African Americans in Colorado and throughout the Rocky Mountain West, it is one of only five such libraries in the country and includes specialized archival documents and a museum. The three-story building is named after Omar Blair, the first Black president of the Denver School Board and Elvin Caldwell, the first Black Denver City Councilperson.

The Stiles African American Heritage Center remains a valuable fixture in Five Points as well. The museum displays cultural exhibits and artifacts of Black achievements and contributions to the American story. Grace Stiles recently celebrated her 90th birthday at her Heritage Center with family, friends and community.

This neighborhood reflects so many different stories that cannot be lost. The beauty of Five Points is in its fascinating heritage. There is passion, there is drive, there has always been a spirit of making the possible out the impossible. There is ongoing strength and sustainability woven through it all.

We must continue to touch and delve into the rich history, the remarkable stories and the amazing traditions. Amidst all the changes, it is vital to not lose sight of where we have been, for that is the only way we can effectively move forward.

Pulling together history and stories like musical notes, blending those unique sounds into an incredible melody – making a beautiful song that the whole world wants to hear. This is how Five Points will live on forever.

Afterword

"The service you do for others is the rent you pay for your room here on Earth."

- Muhammad Ali

Although I have had to say farewell to a number of chapters in my life, from Black radio to promotions, from talk radio to formally creating employment opportunities, all goodbyes are not forever.

I believe there are other opportunities out there that are yet to be created, and I know I will continue to give my voice beyond the 50 plus years I have already been in Denver.

My granddaughter Lindsay, "Miss Thang," said in an interview after I had sold KDKO, "God has something even bigger and better in store for my grandfather. God has not brought him this far to drop him."

I think about her words after each endeavor of my journey has come to its fruition, and it has always been true; God has not brought me this far to not have something bigger and better in store for me. Each chapter of my life is a building block for what is to come. I feel immense gratitude for each experience God has guided me to and through.

I feel a song in my heart for so much that not only has already been, but for what is still yet to be. All the components of my life that have made me who I am are continuing to create space for more dreams, more aspirations, more accomplishments, more hope; opening doors for what is ahead, with love and unity.

Only you know the particular song that resides in your own heart. I encourage everyone to find the passion that is in your own unique soul. We all have the power to create the story that we would like to be our own, our purpose, our legacy. I hope I have given some glimmer of inspiration through my story and my experiences. Success is rarely a smooth or easy road, but the key is to never give up.

To echo my mother's words: "There is not anything in the world you cannot do. But you've got to have patience. And sometimes, it will take a lot of hard work. And there might be a wait until the time is right."

I had no idea how true those words would become for me throughout my life, with everything I've worked to achieve.

Even if all you can see is darkness around you, never lose faith that there can be sunshine ahead. It is up to each of us to find that light, and to keep it shining bright.

God has something more for me in the wings, and it is in His hands to help take my work to another level. I will always continue to strive for Unity in the Community.

We all have so much to give to the world, each and every one of us.

And for me, it all began with radio in my soul.

Words From My Children

||||ıı||ıı||ı 🎤 ıı||ıı||ıı||ı

In everything I've accomplished, family is at the foundation. Through it all, I have discovered this to be my greatest truth, from the family of my childhood, with my mother, sister and brother, to the family of my adulthood, my wife, my children, my grandchildren, and now great grandchildren. I have five incredible children, all who have achieved greatness in their own right. So, they can share their own stories as they choose, I wanted to give each of them the opportunity to speak in their words about their life growing up with Dr. Daddio as their father.

In addition to Yolanda, Ricky, Michael, Jasmine, and Machelle, I have seven amazing grandchildren: Lindsay, Alexis, Halle, Aryana, Tori, Allen ("J.J.") and Harris. I am also blessed with my four great-grandchildren, Xavier, Levi, Josh Jr., and Naomi. All of them help to keep my own bright light shining.

Yolanda Walker

It was exciting growing up with James "Dr. Daddio" Walker as my dad. Our immediate family was small, but our lifestyle was grand, from family gatherings to backyard BBQ's, from RV trips to social events. We had just about every entertainer of the era at our home, record shop, motor home, or special event, from James Brown, Rick James, Tina Marie, The Temptations, Johnny Taylor, and a host of others. There were very few entertainers we didn't know on a first-hand basis.

One thing that amazed me, then and to this day, is no matter where I go in the country and abroad someone can tell me a story on how Daddy encouraged their lives.

My parents gave us a sheltered life. My circle of friends was very small and remains so to this day. I attended a public school from 1st to 9th grade. Then, from 10th through 12th grade, I attended a private school. The popularity of my parents made them extremely cautious. I remember at 9th grade continuation; I was set to follow to public high school with other kids in the neighborhood. My mother stated I didn't have an option to attend public school anymore. I couldn't wait until Daddy got home because I just knew Daddy wasn't going to agree. Besides, I needed a social life! Well, Daddy did agree, and said, "Yo, it's for your own good. You'll thank us later in life." That was the first time Daddy ever told me "No." Later in life I did understand.

Thank you again, Mommy and Daddy, for teaching me a solid education means more than popularity!

One of my favorite memories growing up as the daughter of Dr. Daddio is the day he came home and announced, "The Jackson 5 are coming to Denver." I couldn't believe it! Daddy, being a concert promoter as well as a radio announcer and businessman, was bringing in one of the number one groups of all time! I think every young girl eight to twenty years old was preparing for this concert and yours truly had the inside scoop! If that wasn't enough, four days before the concert he told me I would introduce The Jackson 5 to the stage. I was in shock! I missed a few days of school because my mother and I had to find the perfect outfit to match my daddy's. I had a script to learn and my position on stage, etc. Daddy hired what we know today as a "Glam Squad." They transformed me from an everyday kid to a "Superstar." To this day I remember my mother stating, "Don't make her look grown." Daddy made sure I had my own dressing room, security, and limo; everything was perfect. We practiced so I learned my script like a pro. The days leading up to the show were intense. I realized concert promotion was serious business and my daddy wasn't your everyday kind of dad. This business wasn't for the weak and Daddy was a very strong man.

The night of the show, my mother, Ricky, Michael and I were in my dressing room with my name on the door. Everything was timed to the second; five knocks on the door was my signal. Mom opened the door, holding my hand as we walked down the hall with four security guards, two on each side; we were on our way. My knees were shaking. As we drew closer, we could hear Daddy's voice on stage. I squeezed my mother's hand so hard...she just smiled and nodded. I kissed her and a security guard whisked me to the stage. Daddy's voice was getting louder and louder and the crowds hype was incredible! it was only minutes that I stood in the wings waiting for my cue, but it seemed like hours. Daddy looked to his left and I walked on stage. Our practice had worked to perfection. I looked to my left and saw Mr. Joe Jackson; he smiled and nodded at Daddy. Daddy looked at me and I said, "Ladies and gentlemen, Michael,

Marlon, Jermaine, Tito and Jackie; The Jackson 5!!" The crowd went crazy!! We all smiled at each other as we exited, and the show was on. It was the best concert ever; my very own party with the Jackson 5!! Later, I received a Diana Ross doll. To this day, I have no idea who sent it. All I know is it had a Hollywood return address.

Thank you, Daddy, for that special night I will never forget!

Later in life, I realized Daddy was a visionary. My two daughters, Lindsay and Alexis, and I were driving home with my dad from a trip to Louisiana. Daddy looked at an open area in the middle of nowhere and asked, "What do you see?" The three of us looked at him like he had been driving too long, all of us seeing the same open field. We asked him what he saw. He told us he saw homes, stores, and a community. A few years later, we were traveling to Louisiana, and to my amazement, exactly what Daddy had seen was there. From that day on, I believed if you could visualize it, it could become reality.

Thank you, Daddy, for giving me a vision!

RVing was a big get-away for my family. It was my parent's way to relax, and Daddy loves to fish. We started with a small overhead camper which has now led to a luxurious Class A coach fit for a king. It is special because it gives Daddy an opportunity to share with children, grandchildren, and now great-grandchildren.

Thank you, Daddy, for that special legacy!

The proudest moment was when I received the call from Daddy saying, "The deal is done. We are the proud owners of KDKO radio." He had already owned a station in Arizona. There was never a doubt in my mind that he could complete the deal. My dad could do anything. Five Points would be the home, the slogan "Power 1510

KDKO." The kicker was "Unity in the Community." And I loved "You better ask somebody!"

I am so proud of my dad for having the vision to move KDKO into Five Points. When we walked into the space above Wells Fargo Bank, we were like, "Really, this building?" It was an open area without any walls. We built the studio, the offices, and the amazing space it became. He didn't just talk the talk, but he walked the walk. It was an older building, but when you walked up those stairs, it was one of the most beautiful radio stations in the country, and for it to be Black-owned and family operated. It let our culture know that someone still cares. It was very fitting that the basement of the building housed Paul Stewart's original Black American West Museum.

You don't see a lot of activists walking the walk anymore and making a difference. Entertainers would literally be on that corner on Welton Street shaking hands with people in the neighborhood. Daddy was the type of brilliant promoter that if a star is going to come to Denver, they are going to interact with people. The artists would get off the plane and come to the studio for an interview. It was all about letting people know you were there, letting the audience know you were in town, and then in turn selling more tickets.

Daddy's dedication to the community opened doors for other Black individuals in Denver and Colorado, such as Mayor Wellington Webb and Lieutenant Governor Joe Rogers. Daddy helped people realize how much their votes counted, and how important it was to vote these public officials into office. He also paved the way for other Black businesses, Black Dollar Day, Double Dose Tuesday, and so much more. Daddy coordinated countless youth fishing trips,

KDKO food drives, Christmas toy drives, and school supply drives
Thank you, Daddy, for giving back to the community!

Growing up, we had rules and regulations. There was discipline not just for our family, but for the kids in the neighborhood. Daddy would get on them just like they were his own. He taught me to do my best, respect others, work hard as no one owes me anything, and never forget where I came from and the shoulders I stand on. Always give back, and it will be given back to you.

I can't talk about my dad without talking about my mother. She was the most beautiful woman, inside and out. She was one of the best-dressed women there has ever been. She was strong but kind, and she was very intelligent. When I was young, she was Mommy, and as I grew up, she became Mom. She was my best friend and my confidant. She taught me kindness, appreciativeness, and understanding. My mother was LOVE. She stood for what was right. She was the driving force behind Daddy. He was the head of the family, but my mother was in control; Daddy made decisions, but everything went through Mom. She had a special way of communicating. Whether she liked someone or not, she was kind to them either way. No matter what I asked, she had an answer and usually she was right. She was a Southern lady, and she knew how to carry herself at all times. Most people didn't know how powerful she was. She was not one to play with! Behind every great man is a greater woman and that was my mother, Patsy Walker.

I love you; I miss you. You are our queen. Thank you, Mommy, for loving Daddy!

I started working at my mother's record shop when I was very young.

Mom and Dad taught me to run the business. I could count money, make accurate bank deposits, read and understand contracts, and negotiate. At the same time, my parents made sure I had a childhood that included bikes, games, sleepovers, vacations, etc. I had a great childhood.

Thank you, Mommy and Daddy, for making sure nothing was missing from our lives!

I would not trade my daddy for anything in the world. He has worked hard for everything, he has provided for our family, he has protected us, he's a showman, and he is so Blessed.

Thank you, God, for choosing me to be James "Dr. Daddio" Walker's daughter!

James "Ricky" Walker, Jr.

I worked at KDKO for 15 years, and I was known as the "Mystery Man." The internship program my dad ran was amazing. I was honored when my dad made me program director at the station. KDKO had widespread listeners; Cats from the prison in Canon City would call, or send me letters, asking me to play certain records. They would be allowed to listen to the radio for a certain amount of time each day. My mom used to wonder who was accepting the collect calls that weren't specified on the phone bills back then. I've worked at UPS ever since the station was sold, for the past 18 years.

It was greatness having Dr. Daddio as my father. Without him I wouldn't have the things that I have. He has stick-to-itiveness. He is a super visionary. Someone might look at a hill and see dirt, and Dr. Daddio will see a hotel or a Starbucks. Unity in the Community is who he is.

My pops is a disciplinarian through and through. I remember being disciplined often with his no-nonsense attitude. His logic was very powerful: 'If I give it to you, you'll tear it up; but if you buy it, you'll take care of it;' 'If you act this way on the street, people won't give you a pass;' 'If you want to play football, you have to go to practice;' 'Do your homework, so you can get through school.'

My dad has always reminded me of my great grandfather who would teach us how to drive when we were eight or nine years old, sitting on his lap. I have so many memories of my father, no favorites because they have all been great. Growing up, my siblings and I would play in the Dahlia Shopping Center. I really remember my mom's record store in the Dahlia, Pat's Record Parlor. My dad used to play the records at the socials for the neighborhood kids. He would give the kids at the school the singles; the 45s.

When I was a kid, Daddy would take our family camping. He did a youth fishing trip every year – Dr. Daddio's Fishing Club. All the neighbors would participate or support, and everyone would buy reels for the trip. I always had to cover my father's blue's show from 3 to 6 p.m. when he would be gone on the fishing trips, or other places, and I always enjoyed the radio work. Wellington came on at 10:30 a.m., then Thierry Smith had his sports rap, and I came on from 12 to 6 p.m. on Saturdays on KDKO.

I remember well how James Brown would walk down Welton Street with my dad and talk about what was happening to Five Points. He would remind everyone about how Black entertainers used to always play in the Points on Welton. James Brown talked about gentrification and saw what was happening before everyone else did, and before it started happening all over the country in every major city. When they dedicated the James Brown Soul Center of the Universe Bridge in Steamboat Springs and he came on the radio, he didn't want to talk about that, he wanted to talk about Denver and Five Points.

One of the greatest things I remember is one of the big anniversary parties of the station. It was quite an event. I remember too how dad once drove us in the limo to a concert in Kansas City.

My mom was Queen Fashion. She was a special cook, and she would cook for all our friends. She never judged anybody. My mom wasn't a disciplinarian; it was always, "Wait 'til I tell your dad." Mom was super. Mom and Dad would tell the other parents in the neighborhood to discipline us, whup us if they needed. It takes a village. My parents would always have to meet our friends' parents. Kids don't have that sense of community anymore, but my parents instilled that in us.

I'm a nature guy, thanks to my dad. And I'm still a work in progress. My dad may have his flaws, but all I see is greatness.

Michael Walker
Growing up with Dr. Daddio as my father has made me feel like a celebrity's child. It definitely has its ups and downs. People are either excited or resentful. There are sometimes perks involved, and other times people are jealous or threatened.

My dad always kept us grounded so we never got a big head. What stands out for me about KDKO is that it was the first R&B station in Denver. My dad has always been such a visionary. He went to KDKO when it was a country station. For him to have the foresight to know that R&B could become so popular in Colorado was incredible.

I admire so many things about my dad. I think my dad is one of the greatest men to live in the city of Denver, in the state, and beyond. My dad has made an impact and changed so many lives. All the contributions he has made are so far reaching. People will know who I am, and I don't know them. They tell me how my dad has inspired them.

People have often told me I have big shoes to fill, and I feel like doing that would be impossible. I tell people if I could just wear one of my dad's shoes, I would be doing so much better than a lot of people. If I could be even half the man my dad is, I feel I'd be doing better than 80% of the people in the world.

A lot of people think my dad is firm and strict, and he is those things. However, a lot of people don't know about his sense of humor. He has taught me so many things in life. He taught me how to be comfortable in being alone through spending time in nature with him. Fishing is a solitary activity. Even though I like other's company and I am blessed to have a wife, two children and two grandchildren, I also enjoy spending time alone, whether outdoors or at a movie, thanks to the confidence in myself my dad instilled in me. I have Dad's optimism – "The sun is out and it's a beautiful day."

My dad prepared me to be a man and be successful in life. He taught me that when you go places, always bring a pencil and paper. That preparedness has gotten me far in life. I feel like that sage advice once got me a managerial position by just having my notebook in hand.

The list of his teachings goes on: shake hands firmly; look a person in the eye when you talk to them; mean what you say and say what you mean. All this wisdom on becoming a better man I attribute to my dad. Even though my dad is very much about the community and "pro-Black," he never taught me racism or prejudice. The idea that the white man keeps you down was never taught in our house. "If you get an education, you can make your own job," is what I learned instead.

Dad modeled a strong work ethic for his kids. He provided his sons jobs through his businesses, along with our friends and the community. I remember the SWEPCO asphalt sealant was grueling work. To this day I work hard, often feeling like I work circles around millennial guys. He taught us that you never know where a job opportunity may lead, so be the best you can be at whatever it is you do - whether your job is shoveling cow dung or the president of a Fortune 500 company.

He has instilled in all his children the importance and skills to be entrepreneurs, and to have a positive hustle. Education is my background, teaching math and English. When I was working in the school system, kids would ask me what my hustle was; expecting to hear something in a negative light that they associated with a "hustle." I would tell them I pick up scrap metal. There is so much to be found, and it is worth a lot of money. "Don't be destructive, be constructive" - those things I attribute to my dad.

He conveys to us that wisdom and teaching go both ways. The story of pheasant hunting with my dad when I was about 13 years old, reminding him that his mother is still with him even if she passed has always stayed with me. What stands out for me was the look in my dad's face. The soul may leave but the spirit stays here. He knew it but he thought his son was so profound. I will always remember that, and how special I felt that I could help him.

Another favorite memory is when my parents moved to Arizona, driving a big moving van with the contents of their life in Colorado. In the back of the van were my few belongings in comparison, my suitcase, my stereo, and a microwave. They dropped me off at college in Pueblo on their way. It was a symbolic new beginning and a new chapter for all of us.

I don't tell too many people that James Brown is my Godfather – only people I am really close to. They wouldn't believe it anyway – until now!

My Dad figured out how to always make people say "yes." He is very persuasive in a business way, and he never takes no for an answer. My dad taught me to never take "short cuts." Yes, it might save time in the long run, but the work can lose integrity with the risk of a sub-par product. It is always best to put in the work that is required to get the best results. I am reminded of a story from when he was a boy; he had to take some debris out to the barn, and he decided to throw it in a little hole inside the barn just to hide it. It bounced back and almost cut off his toe! I often tell myself taking more steps, even if it's harder, is always better than fewer steps with no toes. His voice echoes in my head with the advice, "I'd rather you not do it at all, than do it half-ass!"

My mom was an amazing woman and she complimented him. My dad is self-motivated, but he needed a strong woman like my mom. She was bright, an accountant with several businesses of her own. She was his queen. Mom could stand alone, but they made a great pair. The greatest contribution my mom made was she showed my dad the power of God and church. She passed away two days after their 60th anniversary. That shows how devoted she was to my dad.

I've seen my dad get a lot of awards and to say that I am proud of him is an understatement. The proudest I have ever been of him though is when he joined the church and became a deacon. To see him enter in front of the congregation professing his love of God was a moment I will always remember, thanks to my mom showing him the power of spirituality.

Jasmine Walker

I'm a hair stylist, and it is so much my passion. It's like my dad says, "If you are doing what you love, you will never work a day in your life." It also gives me the flexibility to take care of my dad. That is my top priority.

My dad is my hero. I am still looking for that Superman. And it falls back to there's only one Superman, one Batman, and my dad is all of those to me: my Superhero.

Honestly, it's always been a little annoying having such an iconic father. Everybody sees "Dr. Daddio," but I see "Dad." What they hear from him, I hear every single day. I am very protective of my dad. One example of this is when Dr. Daddio is teaching you something, I feel you need to appreciate it to the fullest. He has so much knowledge and wisdom to share.

I am the youngest of five. I was the wild, shy kid – my mom would introduce me as her "wild child." If my dad was talking to somebody, I would hide behind him, or I'd be by my mom. In pictures with my dad when he was with some celebrity, you'd see them shaking hands and the caption would say, for example, "(Celebrity's name), Dr. Daddio and his daughter, Jasmine." People would ask, "Where's his daughter?" Then you see this figure behind him in the background, almost like a ghost.

I'd be with him at the store, for instance, and he would introduce me as his daughter. At 16 years old, I didn't want that because once people knew him as "Dr. Daddio" and not James Walker, then I felt like perceptions of me shifted. I feel they would often think I was rich, spoiled, or a "sour patch" kid – like that brand of candy that starts out sour and turns out to be sweet. I consider myself to be a funny, cheerful person, but the initial impression might be based only on an assumption. People seem to often assume fame brings negativity. No, I'm just Jasmine, that's just James - that's Daddy.

Other than that, he is the most magnificent person in the world. You couldn't ask for a better dad, or a better person to be around. Whenever I ask him about something, I may hear the whole story, but I get all the information I want, and I always get what I need.

He missed out on certain things because he was doing so much for other people. For instance, every year my dad would take a group of young men on fishing trips and occasionally an event like that would conflict with something else. He was a mentor to so many and as I grew up, I had to learn to share him, and I came to realize the importance of what he was doing. Over the years, I have run into some of these youth who are now adults. They will tell me what a difference Dr. Daddio made in their lives and how much what he did meant to them, and I can even see the excitement in their eyes. I'm happy that I have shared him with the world. Now, he takes my son fishing, as well as his other grandchildren. He is such a part of all their lives.

I am so fortunate that my dad has been big in his children's lives since we took our first breaths. I have always had both parents and my mom and dad together. When I was younger and I'd wake up, they were right there; when I went to school, they were right there. I feel so blessed that I had them both with me so consistently, while they both touched so many other hearts and lives.

When I told my parents I was going to join the church, they were thrilled, but I told them I didn't want to speak when I went up front so I asked my dad if he would speak for me. He looked at me rather incredulously, but he did. I have such an expressive person for a father, and I have stage fright. I told him that he could say I asked him to speak, and he did. The best people to talk for me are the people who know me the best, my parents. Dad will do whatever I need him to do, as long as it is the right thing.

Dad is a wonderful provider. As I said, he is not just a father, but a hero - my hero. My dad was always here, but because he was a very well-known man, he was always busy; he worked and worked. When I was a little girl, I would often nap underneath his desk at KDKO.

I confess, I never liked the Martin Luther King Marade because we had to walk so far. However, it became our special time together. Every year, I prepared myself for the length of the Marade and I knew I would have so much fun, regardless. I would get to hold my dad's hand and march. Even at 17 and 18 years old, I was still getting up to have that special time with my dad, and to be seen with him. It made me proud.

I was six or seven years old, and we had been at a radio station party. I had my fake fur coat. It felt like we were the true Kardashians; to me that coat was real fur. My Dad had driven us to the party in his limo. He stopped drinking when I was young, and then he would always drink orange juice and grenadine. After the party, the police pulled us over in the limo for no reason except that he was a Black man. Here was this big, beautiful Black man getting out of his own limo in his tux with his ruffled shirt, and his wife all bedazzled. My Dad was hiding his anger that he was pulled over, he has no tolerance for ignorance. The officer had no idea there was an innocent child in the backseat watching all of this unfold. I did not know what racism was at that time. To me, it was like a villain taking down Superman, or the Joker harassing Batman. Seeing my dad go through that gave me the seeds of knowledge to raise my son as a Black man. The police asked if my mom was able to drive and my mom was the one who had a few drinks at the party. No ticket, but they had her get in the driver's seat. Even though there was so much seriousness to what happened that night, over the years we turned it into a family joke; that they thought Mom would be the one to drive, when Dad was the one who did not have an ounce of alcohol. What happened that night made me appreciate my dad even more and made him even more my hero.

I don't love my mom, I'm in love with my mom. She has always been a goddess to me. My mom was the coolest and the funniest person ever. She would tell jokes that would have me rolling. She was absolutely amazing. Mom gave my dad a lot of her dreams so he could have his dreams. But in those dreams, she was always there. He never excluded her out of anything. Mom was a wonderful teacher with so much knowledge. I'm glad I chose both of them from the heavens to be my parents. Out of our family, Dad had the longest relationship with Mom and we can't compare anyone else's to that. Time-wise though, I had the shortest. My memories of her include all the stories I have heard, as well as my own priceless experiences. She's my best friend and I still talk to her. On days that I feel lost, she is always with me; it may not be physically, but I feel her spiritual presence all the time. She is still so included through her memory in our lives. My mom made my dad; she made my hero who he is.

Machelle Walker-Juniel

I would describe my dad as a very high achiever and very passionate about anything he's involved in. He started so many businesses in Colorado, besides his radio station. He always persevered and he made quite a name for himself.

It was an inspiration for me down here in Texas with my mom and myself. My father encouraged a lot of things that I wanted to achieve. The ups and downs he went through helped me realize that I could get through many challenges by his example. He always shared with me his various highlights and experiences. Throughout both childhood and adulthood, I would discover more and more things we had in common, large and small. Our relationship as father and daughter has continued to become even closer over the years. It's amazing how when you become an adult, you realize the wisdom you have always received. He and I are always transparent with each other, and we hear each other out even if we disagree on some things.

When you're young you don't really know all the attributes of your parents. Dad would always share what he was doing and the news on his end. I didn't realize all of what he truly accomplished until I became an adult, and it was so inspirational to see all the things he really achieved in Colorado.

Although I was growing up in Texas, he was such an integral part of my life. I would visit him in Colorado and had a chance to experience seeing him in action with KDKO. He would also come and visit me in Texas. I was always keeping up with what he was doing and keeping it all in perspective in Houston.

I remember coming out to Colorado to visit and it was my first experience with snow. It was so cold! I had a taste of all the functions he was involved in, as I got to experience them as well. He always had so many accolades from those around him, and that just kept growing.

One of my favorite memories is when he came down for my high school graduation and he asked me where I wanted to go to celebrate. I told him the Shamrock Hotel. That was my first experience with a Shirley Temple. Even with it being a non-alcoholic drink, I felt so grown up. I just wanted to have that drink; it sounded so neat. He made sure I was able to have it and enjoy that entire special evening.

I am an educator like my aunt Me-Me was (Dad's sister, Minnie). One year, Gibsland was honoring the oldest members in the community, those over 90 years-old, at an event called the Aging Gracefully Banquet. My aunt was a runner-up for the oldest person as she was 96 at the time. Dad and I made plans to surprise her. He flew to Texas from Colorado, and then we drove together to Louisiana. We brought her two dozen roses. Aunt Me-Me had no idea we were coming, and just to see the happiness and excitement on her face when we walked in with the bouquet of flowers. It was priceless.

She said, "That looks like Buster, and that looks like Machelle."

"Surprise!"

It was just so nice to know how the community felt about my aunt. That was a really nice event and such a happy moment. Gibsland had really fallen in love with Me-Me. She was known as "Mother

Dawson," because she was always there for the community. She was such a respected teacher and really the first teacher to integrate the schools down there. We had a wonderful time. My dad was as excited as she was, and so proud of her. And I am so proud of him.

References

pg. 5 | *Black capitalization*: Wong, B. (2020, September 3). Here's why it's a big deal to capitalize the word 'black'. Huffpost. https://www.huffpost.com/entry/why-capitalize-word-black.

pg. 62 | *Sale of Motown*: Capretto, L. (2015, February 24). Berry Gordy explains how a childhood lesson on race influenced his first few Motown albums: what a childhood newspaper job taught Berry Gordy about race. Huffpost. https://www.huffpost.com/entry/berry-gordy-race-lessons-motown-albums_n_6739274. Also, Gordy, Berry (1994). *To Be Loved: The Music, the Magic, the Memories of Motown*. Warner Books. p. 306.

pg. 167 | *Willie Lynch Speech*: Willie Lynch. (2015, March 15). *The Transformational Agenda Magazine*. https://black-pages.com/willie-lynch.

pg. 169 | *Louisiana Tech*: March, S. (2016, November 15). Tech creates scholarship honoring first African-American students. *Shreveport Times*. https://www.shreveporttimes.com/story/news/education/2016/11/15/la-tech-creates-scholarship-honor-first-african-american-students/93794516/

References

pg. 191 | *Jack the Rapper*: Fenwick, T. (2015, July 3). Jack the Rapper: the rise and fall of the world's largest hip-hop gathering. *Fact Magazine.* https://www.factmag.com/2015/07/03/jack-the-rapper. Also, D, D. (2000, February). Jack the Rapper: the father of black radio. www.daveyd.com/articlejackrapper.html.

pg. 193 | *Marvin Gaye*: Climans, K. (n.d.) Passionate facts about Marvin Gaye, prince of soul. *Factinate.* https://www.factinate.com/people/facts-marvin-gaye. Also, Marvin Gaye Official Website: Home. www.marvingaye.net.

pg. 194 | *Gladys Knight*: Papillon, A. (n.d.) Fierce facts about Gladys Knight, the empress of soul. *Factinate.* https://www.factinate.com/people/gladys-knight-facts. Also, Gladys Knight Official Website: Bio. www.gladysknight.com. Also, Gladys Knight. (2022, November 21). *In Wikipedia.* https://en.wikipedia.org/wiki/Gladys_Knight.

pg. 195 | *The Supremes*: Chandler, D.L. (2019, January 15). Little known black history fact: The Supremes. Blackamericaweb.com. https://blackamericaweb.com/2019/01/15/little-known-black-history-fact-the-supremes. Also, The Supremes. (2022, October 25). *In Wikipedia.* https://en.wikipedia.org/wiki/The_Supremes

pg. 196 | *The Temptations*: The Temptations Official Website: History/Bio. www.temptationsofficial.com. Also, The Temptations. (2022, November 23). *In Wikipedia.* https://en.wikipedia.org/wiki/The_Temptations.

pg. 197 | *B.B. King*: IndiaToday.in (2015, May 16). B.B. King: the king of the blues dies at the age of 89: 10 facts you shouldn't miss. *India Today*. https://www.indiatoday.in/education-today. .Also, B.B. King. (2022, November 27). *In Wikipedia*. https://en.wikipedia.org/wiki/B.B._King Also, B.B. King Official Website: About. www.bbking.com.

pg. 199 | *James Brown*: Sullivan, C. (2020, April 25). 15 facts to know about James Brown. *GQ Magazine*. https://www.gq-magazine.co.uk/culture/article/james-brown-facts. Also, Mehroo, S. (n.d.). Musical facts about James Brown, the godfather of soul. *Factinate*. https://www.factinate.com/people/james-brown. Also, James Brown Official Website: Bio. https://www.jamesbrown.com. Also, James Brown. (2022, November 24). *In Wikipedia*. https://en.wikipedia.org/wiki/James_Brown

pg. 200 | *WLAC Radio*: Leimkuehler, M. The untold story of WLAC, the powerhouse Nashville station that helped introduce R&B to the world. *USA Today*. https://news.yahoo.com/untold-story-wlac

pg. 207 | *Wellington Webb*: The honorable Wellington Webb. (n.d.). *The HistoryMakers*. www.thehistorymakers.org/biography/honorable-wellington-webb. Also, Wellington Webb. (2022, November 15). *In Wikipedia*. https://en.wikipedia.org/wiki/Wellington_Webb

pg. 208 | *Wilma Webb*: The honorable Wilma Webb. (n.d). *The HistoryMakers*. www.thehistorymakers.org/biography/honorable-wilma-j-webb. Also, Daniel, S. (2020, January 15). 'My duty': former state rep Wilma Webb's journey to create MLK day in Colorado. *KUNC: NPR for Northern Colorado*. https://www.kunc.org/news/2020-01-15/

my-duty. Also, Wilma Webb. (2022, November 16). *In Wikipedia.* https://
en.wikipedia.org/wiki/Wilma_Webb.

pg. 209 | *Cleo Parker Robinson*: Cleo Parker Robinson. (n.d.). *The
HistoryMakers.* https://www.thehistorymakers.org/biography/cleo.
Also, Cleo Parker Robinson. (2022, July 16). *In Wikipedia.* https://
en.wikipedia.org/wiki/Cleo_Parker_Robinson.

pg. 211 | *Hiawatha Davis*: Portrait of Hiawatha Davis. (n.d.) *Public Art:
Denver Arts & Venue.* https://denverpublicart.org/public-arts/portrait-
of-hiawatha-davis.

pg. 213 | *Les Franklin*: Associated Press. (2000, September 2). 10 years after
son's suicide, father deals with suicide of 2nd son. *Deseret News.* https://
www.deseret.com/2000/9/3/19527022/10-years. Also, Davidson, J.
(2015, April 15). Shaka foundation, like its leaders, operates with love.
The Denver Post. https://www.denverpost.com/2015/04/15/shaka.
Also, The Shaka Franklin Foundation for Youth: About Us. https://
shaka.org.

pg. 214 | *Moses Brewer*: Blankenship, N. (2021, February 9). Black history
month profile: Moses Brewer. *University of Denver: Athletics.* https://
denverpioneers.com/news/2021/2/9/athletics. Also, Glynn, J. (2012,
February 13). Alum Moses Brewer still building relationships at 65.
University of Denver Magazine. https://magazine-archive.du.edu/news/
alum-moses.

pg. 215 | *Lu Vason*: Chawkins, S. (2015, May 23). Lu Vason dies at 76; highlighted role of black cowboys. *Los Angeles Times*. https://www. latimes.com/local/obituaries/la-me-lu-vason-20150523-story.html.

pg. 216 | *Nick Metz*: Schmelzer, E. (2019, October 10). Aurora police chief leaving position on his own terms, but won't completely rule out a return to policing. *The Denver Post*. https://www.denverpost. com/2019/10/10/nick-metz.

pg. 217 | *Reginald Holmes*: New Covenant Christian Church Alpha & Omega Ministries Official Website: About. https://www.ncccaom.org

pg. 221 | *Bee Harris*: Rosalind "Bee" Harris. (n.d.). *Colorado Women's Hall of Fame: Inductees*. https://www.cogreatwomen.org/project/rosalind-bee-harris.

pg. 222 | *Vikki Buckley*: Buckley, Victoria (Vikki) 1947-1999. (n.d.). *Encyclopedia.com*. https://www.encyclopedia.com/.../buckley-victoria-vikki-1947-1999.

pg. 226 | *brother jeff*: brother jeff (n.d.). *One Colorado*. https://one-colorado.org/jeff-fard. Also, brotherjeff.com: Bio. https://www. brotherjeff.com/bio.

pg. 227 | *Five Points*: Mauck, Laura M. (2001). *Five Points Neighborhood of Denver*. Arcadia Publishing. Also, Five Points. (n.d.). *Colorado Encyclopedia*. https://coloradoencyclopedia.org/article/five-points.

Acknowledgments

Special thanks to the two pastors who have most helped shape my adult life.

I send gratitude to Reverend Willie Simmons, formerly of Central Baptist Church, for being instrumental in turning my spiritual life around. His guidance renewed my faith in God that I had grown up with in my young church life, reminding me of that foundation that will never leave me.

And thank you to Reverend DeWayne Moore of Ebenezer Baptist Church for continuing to guide me in his leadership along my ongoing sacred path. He reinforces my faith when my road is challenging, and when it is joyful.

I am grateful for their commitment, love and support. And I pay it forward in their honor.

About the Co-Author

Misti Aas is a free-lance writer and journalist. Over the past 15 years, she has written for several community newspapers including *African American Voice, Denver Urban Spectrum,* and *5 POINTS NEWS.* Misti enjoys capturing stories and sharing narratives, as there is no shortage of important stories to tell. In her early writing career, she published a collection of pet care columns, *Caring for our Companions, Heroes, and Best Friends.* A counselor by training, Misti calls Aurora, Colorado her home.

"I am and always will be a catalyst for change."
- Shirley Chisholm